CHECKPOINT

Published by 404 Ink
www.404Ink.com
@404Ink

Please note: Due to the nature of the subject matter, most engagement with gaming theory is hosted online, with no print equivalent, so many references within the endnotes have had to rely on URLs. All references within endnotes were accessible and accurate as of June 2020 but may experience link rot from there on in.

Editing: Laura Jones & Heather McDaid
Proofreading: Janette Ayachi
Typesetting & interior design: Laura Jones
Cover design: Leah McDowell (ELEMdesign)
Co-founders and publishers of 404 Ink:
Heather McDaid & Laura Jones

ISBN: 9781912489282
ebook: 9781912489299

Printed and bound in Great Britain by Clays Ltd, Elcograf S.p.A.

CHECKPOINT

*HOW VIDEO GAMES
POWER UP MINDS,
KICK ASS AND
SAVE LIVES*

JOE DONNELLY

TABLE OF CONTENTS

If you need someone to talk to Samaritans are a mental health charity and service for crisis and support.

Whatever you're going through, you can contact Samaritans in any way below:

Phone: call from any phone on 116 123.
It's free, one-to-one and open 24 hours a day.

Email: jo@samaritans.org
and they will respond to you as soon as they can.

Write:
Chris,
Freepost RSRB-KKBY-CYJK,
PO Box 9090,
Stirling,
FK8 2SA.

They aim to reply within 7 days.

More information: samaritans.org

CONTENT WARNINGS

- **Anxiety**

  Chapters 1, A New Challenger Appears (page 35 – 41), 5, 8, 9, 10, 11, 12

- **Bipolar disorder**

  Chapter 2

- **Borderline personality disorder**

  A New Challenger Appears (page 115)

- **Depression**

  Chapters 1, A New Challenger Appears (page 35 – 41), 2, 4, 5, 7, 8, 12

- **Miscarriage & fertility**

  A New Challenger Appears (pages 113 – 118)

- **Obsessive Compulsive Disorder (OCD)**

  Chapters 1, 7

- **Post Traumatic Stress Disorder (PTSD)**

  Chapters 2, 9

- **Self-harm**

  Chapter 7

- **Sexual assault, trauma & rape**

  Chapters 1, 2, 5

- **Substance use & addiction**

  Chapter 4, 6, 10

- **Suicide**

  Introduction, A New Challenger Appears (page 35 – 41), chapters 3, 4, 5, 7, 10, 11, 12, 13

A NOTE ON SPOILERS

Discussing video games and media means sometimes discussing all elements of them, including endings and pivotal narrative moments. *Checkpoint* will occasionally engage with video game endings, which may include spoilers for some readers. I have tried to the best of my ability to provide markers where there may be spoilers and where you can continue reading without anything being revealed.

Look out for this message in-text:

(⚑ *Spoilers! Skip to the next little flag to avoid.*)

There will be another flag icon in the following paragraphs or pages which indicates where you can safely continue reading.

If you wish to experience any of the games in this book for yourself, go to page 263 where you can find all games mentioned in one comprehensive list, including the platform, whether PC, console or mobile.

FOREWORD

When I first prepared the pitch for a book that celebrated the benefits of video games on mental health in early 2019, I knew exactly what I wanted from the project, what I wanted it to say and how I was going to write it. I had written about video games and mental health on several occasions previously, in various publications, as both areas are close to my heart, for reasons you will soon discover. At one point during my career as a video games journalist, I had a monthly column for *VICE* which explored both subjects and their complex intersections, which was great, but I wanted to be able to add a bit more of me and my own personal experience. I wanted to tell my story, to map out my journey, its highs and lows, to help others and encourage them to share their voyage with this concept. I wanted to dig into how video games have and continue to support me through dark times, while helping me better understand mental illness – concerning myself, and in a wider contextual sense – and in doing so, I wanted the book to explore some of the independent and mainstream games on the market which either represent or are inspired by, a range of complex mental illnesses.

I was delighted when the publishing company 404 Ink were interested in my pitch and wanted to publish in May 2020. I could not wait to get started. Then I quickly realised what might be obvious to most – there's a big difference between writing a 1,500-word feature article about a single game for a website and writing a book of near 300 pages about my life and the lives and work of gamers; developers, publishers, writers, health professionals and more. No pressure. While I'd always loosely used my first-hand experiences with depression and anxiety to frame my journalism, the need to dig into very personal and difficult past experiences to guide a whole book's structure was much harder than I expected. In all ways. As difficult as it's been to revisit moments and memories from the last few years, getting those words down on paper have been worth it, and I hope you will think so too by the last page.

I submitted my final draft of *Checkpoint* to 404 Ink on Thursday, March 5th, 2020. I received a lovely typeset proof by Monday, March 9th. And, with only a handful of checks, nips and tucks left to go, the book was on-schedule to go to print in April to be released into the world in early May. Two weeks after receiving my typeset proof, the United Kingdom, following numerous other countries around the world, went into lockdown as a result of the novel coronavirus pandemic, COVID-19.

Overnight, everyone in my corner of the world in Glasgow, Scotland was forced indoors, to distance themselves from friends and family and avoid a disease predicted to potentially kill millions if not controlled. The hardships some people have endured through not being able to see loved ones and carers for an extended period of time has been unimaginable. Lockdown has been an essential preventative measure but it will have, and is already having huge impacts on health, both physical and mental, as unemployment soars, a recession worse than the Great Depression looms, and, most heart-wrenchingly, children, parents and grandparents die in busy hospitals, alone, mourned via long-distance video call funerals, attended in-person by a strictly restricted gathering only in the single numbers. By this stage, around 10 weeks into lockdown, most people I know have some kind of connection with someone who has been sick, or who has lost a loved one during the most controlled stretch of quarantine, unable to spend their final moments together.

The mental quandaries during this time cannot be underestimated. The people fortunate enough to keep regular working hours have been forced into irregular working-from-home regimes. Those furloughed under the UK Government's Job Retention Scheme have been, in essence, pushed into mandatory employment breaks with nowhere to go. And those who have been made redundant are jobless during a time when most employers are not hiring. My girlfriend Jenny and I were lucky enough to land in the first category, but with a toddler to entertain, and a surprise pregnancy thrown into the mix, our work/life balance has hardly been straightforward.

When the world went into lockdown, with international flights and holidays being cancelled for the foreseeable future, the role of video games at home came into sharp focus for a route to escapism. Suddenly, sun hats and flip flops had to be replaced with consoles and controllers. Virtual worlds offered entertainment in ways reality couldn't, something underscored by the fact that games such as *Call of Duty*, *FIFA*, *Overwatch*,

Candy Crush and *World of Warcraft* reported player-number spikes of several million during the first few months of global stay-at-home orders.[1] With schools temporarily closed in some countries, kids escaped into the digital playgrounds of *Fortnite* and *Minecraft*; and parents, who may have otherwise ignored the medium entirely during normal circumstances picked up a control pad and took the time to understand the online worlds within which their children so often explore and socialise.

I finished writing *Checkpoint* before COVID-19 took grip, but in the light of the coronavirus crisis, the position of recommending video games to help cope with, balance or improve mental health became all the more relevant. Isolation is often a central tenet of mental illness, not least the depression and anxiety disorder I live with myself, and thus at a time when self-isolation was enforced, the importance of tools which can help alleviate these conditions became vital in that process.

Whether it be Zoom call quizzes with family and friends, reliving your childhood in games like *Sonic Mania*, reinventing yourself on your private island in *Animal Crossing: New Horizons*, or becoming one of the nearly 900,000 players who became virtual coaches during *Football Manager*'s two-week free trial period in March. Over 600,000 people who'd never played *FM* contributed to the 21 million matches played and 40 million goals scored[2] – a new precedent was set for gaming in many households in Scotland, the UK and beyond. With mental health in mind, *Football Manager* also changed all of its in-game advertising to promote mental health charities during its free trial, which was a nice a touch, and was also forced to sidestep a third complimentary week at the advice of British emergency services who had noticed a sizeable dip in internet bandwidth in certain areas of the country.

In these uncertain times, there are of course more important things than book delays. While the publication of *Checkpoint* has been pushed back by a few months, its main message still stands and only gets stronger with time. Maintaining sound mental health is the most important thing to me, and I strongly believe, now more than even when I handed in the manuscript, that video games can educate, inform and hold our hands as a tangible coping mechanism. Let me be clear: I am not a mental health professional, nor a video game developer, which is why I've spoken to those better qualified in these areas throughout *Checkpoint* to complement my personal experiences. I hope you enjoy it and continue to stay safe, physically and mentally; wherever you are in the world, however the 2020 pandemic touched you.

Joe Donnelly
June, 2020

INTRODUCTION

A PLAYER HAS LEFT THE GAME

From the front door, I could hear my mother laughing. Then I realised she was crying. Not only was she crying, but she was also bawling – inconsolably roaring from her bedroom upstairs – as my father greeted me at the door. I stepped into the hallway and he forcefully ushered me into the living room, my mind struggling to comprehend what was going on. Nobody likes to see their parents upset, but there was something particularly unsettling about hearing my mum so audibly grief-stricken from another room. I didn't see her face, her stare, or her tears, and yet I created an image in my head and I will never forget it.

Later, I learned that my mum avoided my return home that day to gather some composure while my dad relayed the news to me, but instead of the calm she hoped for, her momentary absence had caused her to break down. She'd received the news that morning, you see, and had to wrestle with it all day. I, on the other hand had been at work, and then up at Strathclyde University to sit an entrance exam for an English Literature degree course I'd later get accepted onto but would never actually start.

My dad sat me down in the living room, the evening sun beaming through its bay windows. He quietly said, 'Your uncle hanged himself today.'

★ ★ ★

On May 12, 2008, Jim Brown, my uncle, killed himself. No matter how many times I write that sentence down it still shocks me. That moment from twelve years ago, at the time of writing, set me off on my mental health journey, one which has delivered a handful of highs, a fair number of lows, and an inadvertent, but enlightening, degree of self-discovery.

I've learned a lot from books, film and television in my quest to understand the depression and anxiety I now struggle with; brought on, so say doctors, by the brutal nature of my uncle's death. I'm also an avid video game player, and while becoming a fully-qualified plumber and gas-fitter upon leaving school in my late teens, I've since retrained as a fully-qualified journalist who once specialised in writing about video games. I did so because the interactive and persuasive nature of video games allows the medium to engage and inform on a level that the traditional media I listed above, simply cannot.

Reading, watching television and listening to the radio are all examples, I believe, of two-dimensional activities. The person on the telly – the newsreader, the actor, the documentary maker – tells you something; you listen, you watch, you consider the information and, most likely, move on with your day and forget all about it. Video games, on the other hand, require you to engage on a multi-dimensional level. Imagine turning your game console on, watching your chosen game load up, and then placing your control pad on the floor. That game isn't going anywhere without your input, and for that frozen screen to move, or to progress through the game's story, to understand whatever it wants to tell you, *you've* got to make it happen. The game tells you something, you listen, you watch, you consider the information, and then *you* make *it* move on. All of which puts video games in a unique position to explore interpersonal themes – such as my focus on issues of mental health, including suicide, depression, and a wealth of other sensitive and complex subject matters – by virtue of player agency.

Before we continue, let me first ask you a question: are you a gamer? You might be, you might not be, and you might not realise you are. If you play video games, you're a gamer. Simple as that. Maybe your Friday night consists of a few beers and a game of *NBA 2K20* on the PlayStation 4 with some basketball-loving pals; or perhaps you play *Fortnite: Battle Royale* on your PC with random folk online. Perhaps you play *Super Mario Odyssey* on a Nintendo Switch handheld while sprawled out on the couch after a hard day at work, or maybe you've scouted every noteworthy rising star in *Football Manager 2020* on your dad's work laptop. (Don't worry, I won't tell. I'm not a grass.)

Maybe your game of choice is animated cooking simulator *Overcooked*, which you play with your significant other on Xbox One. I mean, I say "play", but if you're like anyone I know, I bet your sessions end with you screaming at one another in real life, as your on-screen avatars set fire to the room around them thanks to a neglected pot of overboiled tomato soup. Seriously, if your relationship can survive half an hour with that game then you're in a good place.

Maybe you don't play games on a console, a handheld, a PC or a laptop, but you play *Candy Crush* on your smartphone or you are a *Farmville* veteran. Maybe the effortlessly addictive *Angry Birds* is more your cup of tea, or you're hooked on playing *Coin Master*, *Texas HoldEm Poker* or *8 Ball Pool* on Facebook – the latter of which welcomes 10 million players every month to the game via the social media platform.[1]

If any of this applies to you, then you're a gamer. The internet likes to apply distinctions regarding how serious you take gaming, but luckily most of them are pedantic and don't matter. The most common is the perceived difference between "casual" and "hardcore" players, where people who play games on their phone tend to fall under the former grouping and those who commit more of themselves to the activity land in the latter. Elitism isn't uncommon among those who identify as hardcore gamers, but in 2020, I find the distinction to be false and tired. It's also worth pointing out that just about everyone with a mobile phone – be that a smartphone or anything less sophisticated (I adored *Snake 2* on my Nokia 3310 back in the day) – is a gamer.

One distinction which I would say is relevant, however, is

the one between professional and non-professional gamers. Esports – also known as electronic sports, e-sports, or esports – is a form of sporting competition tied to video games. Esports take the form of organised, online multiplayer video game competitions and tournaments, contested between professional players, individually or as teams. It's a billion-dollar industry,[2] a huge part of modern gaming, with events watched by millions around the world with competitors play for multi-million-dollar prize pools. Naturally, the most successful esports players take video games very seriously. Those people are, to be fair, pretty hardcore.

Besides the pro versus non-pro distinction, though, I don't care much for separating casual and so-called hardcore gamers. Video games should be fun, informative, and inclusive, no matter how often you pick up a control pad, sit in front of a mouse and keyboard, or tap the screen of your phone. And even if you don't feel you fit any one of those profiles, nor consider yourself a gamer by any stretch of the imagination, I bet you know someone who does. I also bet you've crossed paths with video games, inadvertently or otherwise, while consuming other media. In the last decade, video games have improved at exploring the real-world themes covered in the usual media – politics, love, lust, relationships, friendships, depression, suicide, you name it – yet when traditional media aims at video games it can be hit or (a big) miss. For every charming and endearing *Wreck-It Ralf*, there are video game tie-in movies like *Hitman: Agent 47*, *Assassin's Creed* and *Warcraft* waiting to spoil the party.

Perhaps the most interesting depiction of video games in television in recent years is Charlie Brooker's science fiction anthology series *Black Mirror*. Before his TV writing and presenting days, Brooker wrote for the now-defunct video games magazine *PC Zone* in the mid-'90s so he understands the landscape and nuances of video games more than most. To date, the show has aired four episodes that are explicitly about video games – Season 3's "Playtest", Season 4's "USS Callister", Season 5's "Striking Vipers", and a one-off special named 'Bandersnatch'. The latter is a choose-your-own-adventure-style endeavour about a young programmer named Stefan Butler (played by Fionn Whitehead), who dreams of adapting a choose-your-own-adventure book called *Bandersnatch* into a revolutionary adventure video game.

In doing so, 'Bandersnatch' turns the TV show itself into a fully-fledged video game. By inputting binary decisions via their television's remote control, users (players?) can shape the show's outcome via a network of branching narratives. This format of storytelling is synonymous with video games, but, having played it for the first time as it launched in late 2018, it was the first time I'd seen a gaming-like function executed with such finesse on 'traditional' TV. I won't spoil the specifics of the plot because you should try it for yourself ('Bandersnatch' is available on Netflix), but ultimately the user's choices begin pretty lightweight – the first decision to made involves breakfast: Frosties, or Sugar Puffs? – and gradually begin to weigh heavier with each plot twist and fork in the narrative road.

In pursuit of five different endings in 'Bandersnatch', it's possible to make mistakes in your choice selections, which can ultimately drive the story to a dead-end – just like the books that it draws inspiration from. Anyone who grew up in the '90s, like me, will remember the *Goosebumps* horror series' take on choose-your-own-adventure, and will likely also remember how frustrating it was to wind up dead through the process of bad decision-making. The frustration is no different here. Still, 'Bandersnatch' can be dark, funny, and unsettling – at once and at the click of a button – much like many of the video games it strives to reflect.

In conversation with *PC Gamer*'s Andy Kelly shortly after 'Bandersnatch' was released, Brooker himself said a common criticism of the episode was that video games have been using player-driven branching narratives for some time, and they now do so in more sophisticated and complex ways, to which Brooker's reply was: 'Yeah, they are, but they're not running on Netflix. This is not a gaming platform!'[3]

Which is, of course, what stands 'Bandersnatch' apart, placing it in this curious limbo between television and video games, tentatively bridging the gap between passive and interactive entertainment. Despite praise from some facets of the media that said 'Bandersnatch' was a new form of storytelling, Brooker disagreed – 'It's basically [Rick Dyer and Don Bluth's 1983 video game] *Dragon's Lair,* but a different iteration of that' – but he did admit that if people play his creation and like the idea of interactive storytelling, it may lead them to try something more advanced. Something more advanced would be video games, wouldn't it? If you were taken by 'Bandersnatch''s gamified methods of engagement, there's a whole universe of video games out there that take the concept and stretch it further than you could imagine. Whether you're a hardcore gamer, a newly enlightened casual gamer or a straight-up non-gamer (I'll convert you yet), you'll have been affected by video games in some way.

* * *

One of the most interesting and satisfying things about my experiences writing about video games and mental health for the *Guardian*, *New Statesman*, *Telegraph* and *VICE*, among others, is the fact that doing so has prompted a number of my close friends to share their struggles with mental health too – and these are stories which might have otherwise gone untold. Hailing from working-class backgrounds in Glasgow, a city privy to an obstructively self-deprecating, self-effacing, *keep yer chin up, pal* culture, I think that's quite remarkable.

Speaking to the BBC in 2018, Andy Przybylski, the Director of Research at the Oxford Internet Institute, who studies how video games impact our mental health, said: 'Nobody is properly talking to each other', in reference to games and mental health.[4] *Checkpoint* aims to pick that control pad up from off the floor and kickstart that discussion through the lens of the biggest and most successful entertainment medium in the world.

To be clear: anyone struggling with their mental health should seek the help of qualified professionals should they be able, but no matter what your own circumstances are, I hope this book speaks to you, or someone you know if you pass it on, or at least helps broaden your understanding of video games and the medium's power to stir emotion and convey information in and around an often stigmatised subject matter. As I tell you about Uncle Jim and the games I played in the aftermath of his suicide, you'll hopefully see a subtle road map of my mental health journey and maybe you'll see yourself on a similar path, or not at all. Whatever you see in this book, I hope you'll take something positive from it.

CHAPTER 1

A NEW JOURNEY

SETTING THE SCENE

I 'll get straight to the point: if no one is talking to each other, then we simply need to start talking to each other. This is especially the case in Scotland, my home, and mental health issues are killing at record levels. Two people take their own lives in Scotland every single day.[1]

Some more terrifying statistics set the scene within just the UK (worldwide analysis on suicide rates is widely available from the World Health Organisation):

Over 5,600 Scottish males have taken their own lives since my uncle's passing in 2008.[2]

680 suicides were registered in Scotland (522 males and 158 females) in the same year.[3]

Scotland had the highest suicide rate in the UK in 2018,

with 16.1 deaths per 100,000 people (784 deaths), a year where males accounted for 17.2 deaths per 100,000 people up and down the country – a trend that's been consistent for 10 years.[4]

The statistic you're probably the most familiar with: Suicide is the single biggest killer of men under 45 in the UK, and 84 men take their own lives every week.[5]

Despite the Scottish national average suicide rate falling more recently, the rate of suicides amongst young men in Scotland increased for the third consecutive year in 2017.[6]

Aye, but it's a coward's way out, says the whisky-nosed man in the pub, who preaches outdated machismo rhetoric about safeguarding stiff upper lip stoicism, and how it's only women and *pansies* who should cry and share their feelings and, heaven forbid, rely on emotional support should they ever need it. Needless to say, that's antiquated bullshit. And the man from the pub is an arsehole.

Oh, but they didn't seem like the type of person that'd kill themselves, says the casual well-wisher, whose would-be wholesome exchanges, bless them, invariably spiral into a blur of blank stares, hollow sentiments and awkward shoe-shuffling. Don't get me wrong, I wish there was a universal profile, a stereotype, a cookie-cutter personality for suicide – if there was, we'd be better equipped to identify and, crucially, help those in need – but there's quite simply not.

Overcoming modern misconceptions, then, is surely as

important as hurdling age-old stigma when it comes to gaining wider mental health discourse. On finding out your uncle has killed himself… how exactly do you process that? The answer is that you don't. At least, not right away.

Instead, you spend the best part of a year grieving, you piss off to Australia for two years to distance yourself from it all, you return and get listlessly consumed by a tidal wave of unresolved emotion and resentment, spend another year trying to come to terms with what the fuck is going on inside your head, consult a doctor and then postpone seeking treatment for another 36 months or so. And only then, six years down the line, do you finally engage with the help on offer. If any of this journey is relatable, I hope you did a better job of managing it than I did.

In my defence, I didn't really know what depression was before my uncle's death. Then 22 years old, I certainly didn't know how to identify it, and I wasn't equipped to articulate how it might, in turn, affect me. After my previously-mentioned journey, I've since taken advice from GPs, I've undergone cognitive behaviour therapy (CBT), and have been on a course of anti-depressant medication for nearly six years. During those times, video games played an equally important role in my coming to terms with it all.

At the time of Jim's suicide, I hadn't long started playing Irrational Games' *BioShock*. Inspired by the dystopian hellscapes of George Orwell, Aldous Huxley and Ayn Rand, the first-person shooter game drops players into Rapture, an underwater civilisation, built by fictitious idealist dictator Andrew

Ryan, designed for the perceived higher echelons of society to live and work free of 'petty morality and government control'. After discovering a DNA-altering, superpower-granting property named ADAM, the world gets hooked, humanity crumbles, and Rapture's addicted citizens evolve into gibbering, drug-addled, zombie-like monsters named Splicers. I felt tenuous links between this game and my harsh reality, the shooter video game doubling as a coping mechanism. Maybe I made a subconscious link between my uncle's death and fighting a race of unbalanced blighters who once sought a better life, but who instead wound up trapped by circumstance. In the years leading up to his passing, Jim embarked on a pretty significant career change into property development which, after accruing a sizeable amount of debt unbeknownst to my family and his friends at the beginning of the global financial crisis, was pivotal in his death. Or maybe I was just looking for a distraction.

Either way, I threw myself into *BioShock* like no other game I had played before. I killed Splicers for fun, and I found bashing their heads in with the game's hulking melee wrench weapon extremely satisfying.

***

Ever since their commercial introduction in the 1970s, video games have told stories. Naturally, technological improvements and innovations over the years have allowed for more sophisticated storytelling – 1972's *Pong*, for example, weaves a less

14

complex narrative than, say, 2018's *Red Dead Redemption 2* – but the transformative nature of games has remained constant. Some of my fondest childhood memories involve me saving the planet from nuclear war in Atari's *Missile Command* (1980). And steering scores of green-haired and blue-robed critters to safety in DMA Design's *Lemmings* (1991). And fighting aliens and multi-coloured dragons in Sega's *Space Harrier* (1985). And sending a certain moustachioed Italian plumber up and down dozens of oversized green pipes in Nintendo's *Super Mario Bros* (1985).

After years of corporate giant dominance during the '90s and the '00s, video games industries entered what is considered a renaissance period of sorts, wherein independent game developers began to break the mould by stepping out on their own. Markus Persson's 2009 open-world sandbox game *Minecraft* is considered by most to be the nucleus of the movement, and the likes of *Braid*, *Limbo*, *Super Meat Boy* and *Journey* were all developed by spirited, innovative and, crucially, self-publishing creators, shortly thereafter.

Over time, this indie renaissance paved the way for video games which consider a whole host of unlikely themes, including mental health. Fullbright's *Gone Home*, for example, explores homosexuality through a series of coming-of-age diary entries. Lucas Pope's *Papers, Please* tackles political hostilities through the eyes of a fictional Eastern-bloc immigration officer. *The Stanley Parable* questions the futility and the illusion of choice through the lens of the daily 9-to-5 grind. *Actual Sunlight* by Will O'Neill is a short interactive story about a dysfunctional 30-something man who struggles with love, depression and societal integration.

Zoe Quinn's *Depression Quest* is a narrative adventure that tasks players with managing mental illness alongside the tenets of everyday life – relationships, jobs and the daunting thought of seeking professional help. Vander Caballero's *Papo & Yo*, on the other hand, is a semi-autobiographical tale that explores the emotional fallout faced by its child protagonist as a result of his alcoholic father. Eli Piilonen's *The Company of Myself* examines the challenges of seeking professional help for the first time. Even unlikely big-budget video games, such as *Fortnite* and *Grand Theft Auto V*, are an equally vital part of the conversation, all of which I'll be later exploring. The video games spectrum is as wide and vast and deep as the digital landscapes they so bountifully portray. Their huge and positive scope is limitless, and the ever-pervasive medium can inspire and delight, teach and inform, influence and impress.

★ ★ ★

Not everyone is as enthusiastic as I am. If you're not familiar with many games from first-hand experience, you'll almost certainly have seen/read/heard some media mogul's opinion (emphasis on 'opinion') that video games are, on the one hand, for children, or – on the extreme other hand – create murderers. Starting with the less harmful end of the spectrum, depictions of video games in news programmes and conservative articles as child's play diminishes their position as a credible source of conveying information. How you choose to enjoy video games is up to you – be it to switch off and relax after a long day with

FIFA, meeting up with pals for a round of *Call of Duty* online, or to learn and explore with some of the games listed previously. But pedalling the common and longstanding idea that they're reserved for basement-dwelling teenagers with bad skin and questionable hygiene is still one of the most common stereotypes. It's not only condescending and archaic but also largely false. The average video game player is 35 years old and has been playing games for 13 or so years,[7] and in 2018, the average Scottish player spent £415 on games, downloadable content (DLCs) – additional levels, character power-ups, cosmetic items etc – and virtual currency.[8] Moreover, the largest single age/gender demographic of video game players in the UK is 15-24 year-old males – making up 14 per cent of everyone playing[9] – which means that the video games medium has quite a different consumer base to what the stereotype-pushers say, and it is in a unique position to inform and educate around adult themes.

At the more harmful end of the spectrum, the mainstream media can have a damning impact on the societal perspective of video games – particularly when mental health issues are folded carelessly into the discussion. Here are a handful of negative but unfounded articles related to video games and mental health that inevitably perpetuates inaccurate stereotypes and causalities:

Did violent video game Call of Duty *spark gun-crazed loner's killing spree? Adam Lanza 'spent hours with game just like Anders Breivik'* – Daily Mail Online (December 15, 2012)

> *Boy, 17, who was 'tortured and buried in a shallow grave over a $500 dispute' met the three teenagers accused of his murder via a medieval video game* – Daily Mail Online (March 28, 2019)

> *Trump wants you to think about video games instead of guns* – CNN (March 8, 2018)

> *Nut Cases' wide swath of destruction / Oakland gang ran 'wild,' killing, robbing at random* – SF Gate (February 10, 2003; within which the opening paragraph identifies *Grand Theft Auto 3* as the root cause)

> *French terrorist played violent video game* Call of Duty *before embarking on brutal killing spree of seven, says wife* – Daily Mail Online (June 1, 2012)

The first of these news stories spanning 15 years relates to the potential motives of Sandy Hook Elementary School shooter Adam Lanza in 2012. Within, the article names Activision's long-standing military first-person shooter series *Call of Duty* as a video game that Lanza played regularly and contains insights from a man named Peter Wlasuk, a plumber who is said to have observed posters of military weaponry in Adam Lanza's bedroom when visiting the Lanza household in Connecticut before the shootings.

The source's only quote from Wlasuk within the story reads: 'The kids who play these games know all about [guns]. I'm not blaming the games for what happened. But they see a picture of a historical gun and say, "I've used that on *Call of Duty*".' Which surely quite explicitly answers the question the article's speculative headline poses.

The second article proposes that the three men charged with the kidnapping, torture and murder of Justin Tsang in Sydney, Australia in 2019 met within the online portion of Taleworlds Entertainment's medieval role-playing game *Mount & Blade: Warband* (2010). The article posits those charged with Mr Tsang's murder did so amid a dispute over $500 AUD. On the face of information contained within the news story, the details of where the men charged with murder met – be that in real life or via a video game – seems irrelevant.

The third article is Donald Trump talking bollocks, and while CNN adopts a semi-critical stance towards the US President, the headline is leading, bordering sensationalist.

Some of the claims in the fourth article, published in 2003, are false, not least the suggestion killing non-playable characters in *Grand Theft Auto* games scores the player points. The article then suggests a gang accused and charged of multiple murders were inspired by Rockstar's enduring 18+ crime simulator series *GTA*. There is no evidence within the article to support this beyond its own conjecture.

The fifth and final article, somewhat similar to the first, attempts to explore the motives of another mass shooting, carried out by Mohammed Merah in the south-west of France in 2012. Here, the article posits Merah's ex-wife, Miriam, to whom he was married to for 17 days, said the pair played violent video games together.

The article quotes Miriam Merah as saying: 'We had many religious conversations, but we spent our time playing PlayStation, including *Call of Duty* and *Need for Speed*… we also watched *The Simpsons* together. We talked a lot and he needed someone to listen.' At no point does the article suggest *The Simpsons* or racing game series *Need for Speed* played a part in Merah's unlawful behaviour.

Of course, none of this should detract from the horror of the killings and criminal behaviour. The assertion that mature video games – those designed for adults aged 18 or above – glorify violence or encourage vulnerable people to commit anti-social behaviour any more than other modern media is irresponsible. It's simply untrue. By questioning the mental state of the perpetrators while citing video games as catalysts, these inflammatory articles also serve to perpetuate the stigmas and stereotypes that surround mental illness and fear.

* * *

When I started writing about video games professionally, I would cite *BioShock* – a game which depicts unstable individuals in a crude and gratuitous, plot-serving manner – as my own unlikely nucleus for viewing mental health through the lens of video games. Irrational Games' hit doesn't claim to explore themes of mental health explicitly, but against my now very personal attachment to the shooter game, it did make me consider how video games portray sensitive subjects in and around the discussion, not least suicide. Challenge lies in separating the medium from ill-informed stereotypes. Like many facets of pop-culture media, video games can too often lean into the idea that mental illness is something to be feared. Frustratingly, this serves to accentuate societal stigma around issues of mental health, and more disheartening still, is the fact that this allegory suggests we should fear the unknown. This is an attitude that's not only reductive by its very nature – why wouldn't we instead strive to understand the unknown – but is also untrue in terms of mental health, with boundless literature and information out there to break the stigma of fear and allow anyone to engage and understand the topic better.

The starkest example of the 'mental illness is unknown therefore scary' trope is that there are a *huge* number of horror games set in asylums or psychiatric institutions. Remedy Entertainment's 2010 action game *Alan Wake* is set in an asylum, as are Red Barrels' 2013 survival horror *Outlast* and DreamForge's 1998 point-and-click adventure *Sanatarium*. Psychiatric hospitals in various states of disrepair feature in several of Team Silent's *Silent Hill* survival horror series (1999 – present), while Jyym Pearson's 1981 eerie graphic adventure game *The Institute* is packed with dated and harmful parlance, even for its time. Access Software's 1990 MS-DOS game *Countdown* provides some similarly obtuse mental health commentary, and Tecmo's 2008 horror venture *Fatal Frame 4* takes place within a decrepit sanitorium. Filled with unpredictable, almost always rage-filled baddies, these are a snapshot of the stereotypical portrayals of mental health institutions and also highlight the misconstrued relationship shared between mental illness and horror. People receiving treatment for mental health issues should not be degraded, far less feared, and their depiction as monsters – be that a metaphor manifest of 'the unknown', or because real world hospitals are associated with illness and death – is cruel, unnecessary and gratuitously misinformed.

Moreover, within these games, the psychiatric establishments in question are often abandoned, its patients are often non-playable enemy characters, their behaviours repeatedly unpredictable, and their nature is usually characterised by lazy traits such as subdued speech, erratic movements, anxious dispositions, and/or hostile tendencies. One of the first characters you meet in *Sanitarium* is a chap who repeatedly bangs his head against a concrete wall until his brow is visibly bleeding. In *Outlast*, journalist Miles Upshur spends the majority of his time wrestling with patients inside the game's Mount Massive Asylum and being force-fed jump scares, unpredictable set pieces serve solely to shock players when they least expect it. And in *Silent Hill 2*, while Brookhaven Hospital is designed to underscore protagonist James Sutherland's deteriorating mental state, it nevertheless regurgitates all of the aforementioned antagonistic stereotypes and clichés around the 'criminally insane' in the process.

Another distinction video games often struggle with in mental health terms, not exclusive to the horror genre, is the difference between suicide; heroic-suicide and heroic-sacrifice. The latter two are almost always tied to plot-progression, and likewise often overlap in a bid to paint their characters as martyrs, or at the very least, noble. In the 1998 Japanese

22

role-playing game *Suikoden,* a Game of Thrones-style king by the name of Barbarossa Rugner gets possessed by an evil entity, rediscovers himself towards the game's finale, and ends his own life to protect the world. Basically, Barbarossa heroically kills himself to salvage the lives of others.

Heroic-sacrifice, on the other hand, is when a character offers themselves so to overcome an obstacle for the greater good. This will sometimes cross over to heroic-suicide depending on the outcome of their plight, it ultimately when a character proclaims they're no longer a scaredy-cat and will now do anything for the cause, even if it means giving up their own life. In Telltale's 2012 interactive and choice-heavy narrative-adventure *The Walking Dead,* it's possible for a whole range of characters to meet their maker in this manner.

That's not to say there aren't wholesome examples of all of the above. In LKA's 2016 non-combative exploration game *The Town of Light,* players visit a gamified version of the real life, but now closed Ospedale Psichiatrico di Volterra asylum, situated in the quaint mountaintop town of Volterra in the Tuscany region of Italy. Once dubbed by locals as 'the place of no return', thousands of patients were said to have been sent there for 'treatment' prior to its closure in 1978 but were instead institutionalised indefinitely. By alternating between present day and 1938, *The Town of Light* tells the story of Renée, a 16 year old who gets institutionalised against her will, via forgotten diary entries that depict the atrocities of the then still functioning institution. The game visits the site's examination rooms, sterile corridors and isolation chambers, and is the result of months of extensive research. The Florence-based game developer having pored over the history books and modelled its in-game structures against the still-standing ruins of the Volterra building itself.

Billed as a 'danger to herself and others' by the powers that be, Renée spends much of her life held against her will by Volterra's nurses and orderlies. She is left in isolation for inhumane periods of time, she is forcefully given electroshock therapy, and, in one particularly harrowing scene, Renée is raped. LKA's meticulous attention to detail accentuates the horror of *The Town of Light's* setting and premise, it taps into the dehumanising nature of these long-outmoded institutions, and uses the connection between horror, mental health and video games, to explore a reality that a number of its players, possibly the majority of its players, will never know. Renée's narrative is fictitious yet was inspired by real events. I'll be talking more about this amazing game's journey in the next chapter.

Bloober Team's psychological thriller *Layers of Fear* is a straight-up horror game that plays into the terror of first coming to terms with mental illness, without ever feeling cheap. Filling the shoes of a secluded painter who is tucked away from society and is progressively overcome with loneliness, the game follows the nameless protagonist's journey as he turns into himself and challenges his own debilitating isolation. Anyone who has ever watched a loved one struggle with Alzheimer's or dementia will likely recognise the steady but subtle ways the central character loses his grip on reality. I couldn't help but be reminded of my own granny's vascular dementia prior to her passing in 1997, and the way it robbed her of her essence before the end.

Polish developer Super Sexy Software's *The Shattering* is another narrative-led horror game that taps into the fear of the unknown, without reverting to stereotype. It tells the story of John, a man who suffers from depression, bipolar disorder and psychosis as a result of traumatic events experienced in his past. Again, relatability is what drives John's unfortunate tale – that everyone can find something in common with him and his thought processes. To ensure this was handled sensitively and constructively, however, SSS consulted with a professional psychiatrist who drew up a character profile for protagonist. Throughout the game's development, its creators researched their subject matter thoroughly, and by liaising with mental health professionals were able to write John as if he were a real person. In doing so, SSS were encouraged to focus on how people act, how people talk, how people talk to others with mental health problems, and how they should interact with them. The game's eponymous title looks at the shattering mind, and what fragments of the past the protagonist wants to recall, and which he wants to forget.

Throughout, SSS's work is underpinned by the idea that everyone and anyone can suffer poor mental health, which in turn informs its horror aspects through possibility, circum-stance and likelihood. If you can identify with John, then what's to say you couldn't ever end up in a similar situation

yourself? Creating horror games without leaning on tired stereotypes isn't impossible, despite how mental health is regularly
portrayed in popular culture. Lucy Morris, an independent
game developer, community builder and researcher felt so
strongly about this very point that in 2013 she created Asylum
Jam, a 48-hour game jam that tasks players with creating
horror games free of potentially harmful tropes. Game jams
are a gathering of video game developers whose purpose is to
plan, design, and create games within a short time allocation,
usually between 24 and 72 hours.

Inspired by a games-news website *Kotaku* article by journalist
Ian Maher titled 'Nobody Wins When Horror Games Stigmatize
Mental Illness', Asylum Jam challenges pop culture's generic
interpretation of mental illness, and suggests that popular
media drives popular beliefs, 'which lead to reinforcement,
adaptation or abandonment of stigmatic views'.[10] In his article,
Maher argues that games have an onus to be more responsible in their depictions of mental illness, and in the wake of
this piece, Morris launched Asylum Jam with just one rule for
development: 'You should not use asylums, psychiatric insti-
tutes, medical professionals or violent/antipathic/[so-called]
insane patients as settings or triggers.' Asylum Jam is normally
held around Halloween and has continued to grow every year
since inception.

In the spirit of Asylum Jam's ethos, games such as *Depression
Quest*, *Actual Sunlight* and Matt Gilgenbach's *Neverending
Nightmares* weave an abject sense of horror into their narra-
tives that is driven by realism – in these instances by depression,

suicide and obsessive compulsive disorder. Each of these games explores idiosyncratic terror as it relates to the developers' own struggles with mental health, and while specific to each author, each scenario is pitched in an accessible manner.

Dontnod Entertainment's 2015 episodic graphic adventure *Life Is Strange* considers suicide through a combined lens of morality and player agency. It's a great example of the three-dimensional learn-by-doing nature games can offer. Here, players assume control of Maxine "Max" Caulfield, a self-conscious adolescent who discovers early on that she can rewind time. In the game's second episode, after a typical amount of time-based arsing about, the magnitude of Max's power comes into its own when she has the chance to save a friend, Kate, from taking her own life. During the scenario, it's made clear that the player has only one chance to save Kate, and if they fail, she's gone forever. By using the 'permadeath' game mechanic in this way – where upon death, in-game characters cannot be revived – *Life Is Strange* creates scope for understanding the permanence of real-life suicide.

★ ★ ★

I can't talk about the societal and internal perceptions of the gaming industry without acknowledging those who actually slave away behind screens for years on a single project as many developers, artists, designers, writers, illustrators, and more, do. Like the film industry, video games too often pander to auteur theory, whereby small groups of individuals are singled out for praise when a game sells well at launch. Esteemed series such as *BioShock* and *Metal Gear Solid* are the work of hundreds, sometimes thousands, of video game developers, yet the heads of these organisations – Ken Levine and Hideo Kojima, in this instance – often soak up praise single-handedly on magazine covers, social media and at events. The public praise might be free-flowing but behind the scenes, things aren't always as rosy.

In video game development, crunch is a problem. 'Crunch' is the final push to finish making a game, which often involves mandatory overtime and unethically long hours. Luckily, crunch is publicly decried today by just about everyone in the industry – to the point where games and mental health charity Take This wrote a whitepaper on its dangerous effects on employees' physical and mental health.[11] Unfortunately, many prominent game developers still enforce crunch culture on their staff, away from the public eye today.

Crunch culture was first exposed to the public at length back in November 2004, when an anonymous blog post titled "EA Spouse" was published online, voiced by the partner of an Electronic Arts employee, and detailed their worsening conditioning as a direct result of crunch at work.[12] EA – the company responsible for the *FIFA* series of football games, among many other titles – were forced to pay out tens of millions of dollars in settlements, after further similar cases surfaced in light of the letter.[13] Crunch was almost certainly a problem in the games industry before 2004, but this was the first high-profile example of the poor working conditions implicitly tied to what many video game enthusiasts would have considered a dream job.

EA was again criticised for adopting crunch culture in 2018, during the development of its action role-playing game *Anthem*. Also in 2018, Epic Games was accused of overworking their employees while creating parts of runaway online hit *Fortnite: Battle Royale*. Similar reports emerged that same year within Rockstar Games – the studio behind *Grand Theft Auto* – when making its western-themed epic, *Red Dead Redemption 2*. The company's San Diego branch came under public fire during the development of this game's forerunner, *Red Dead Redemption*, when similar EA Spouse-style letters appeared online, alluding to mismanagement and discord behind the scenes.[14]

In light of this, video games websites *Kotaku* and *Polygon* have become two particularly trusted outlets for anonymous tippers and whistle-blowers. Speaking to the latter about *Fortnite,* a handful of Epic Games employees admitted to working 70 to 100 hour weeks, being sleep-deprived and drained of energy. One Epic staff member revealed that while they were paid overtime, they worked in a culture of fear, and even described a weekend off work as a 'major achievement.'[15] Crunch culture in any shape or form is dangerous, but what makes it potentially worse in cases like *Fortnite* is the fact that these games exist online (i.e. they are not just one-off games that are released and never touched again aside from patches and pre-planned DLCs), so they are constantly evolving, being iterated on, and are never truly 'finished' per se. In theory, crunch culture risks becoming the norm, which can be said about any online game, or any game that comes with a separate online mode.

When speaking to the press ahead of *Red Dead Redemption 2*'s launch, Rockstar Games co-founder Dan Houser mentioned working 100-hour working weeks on 'several occasions', as if this were a good thing. Rockstar were forced to issue a statement thereafter that clarified this only ever applied to 'senior writing staff' (himself, Michael Unsworth, Rupert Humphries and Lazlow Jones), and that these shift patterns had only applied for three weeks of the game's reported eight year development. Houser doubled down by saying Rockstar employees were never expected to work longer hours than contracted, and anyone that did, had done so because of their passion for the project. In an in-depth report on crunch at Rockstar, published the same month *Red Dead Redemption 2* was released, Kotaku spoke generally about anonymous conversations with its employees, reporting that those willing to chat were split – that they heard a variety of positive and negative stories across the majority of its offices (one of which, Rockstar North, is based in Edinburgh, Scotland).[16]

Again, in conversation with Kotaku, EA employees described 'stress leave' as common during the development of both *Anthem* and *Mass Effect: Andromeda*.[17] Crunch culture is by no means exclusive to big-budget, AAA video game development studios, and has scope to affect indie operations as much as it does the big dogs. But when the most world-renowned companies responsible for some of the world's most successful games employ a culture of fear and unreasonable working conditions, then it's clear something has to change from the top down. Unlike many industries, the games industry does not have a big union presence. Game Workers Unite (GMU) is an organisation that promotes unionisation within the video games spectrum and strives to tackle game development's most dangerous tangent. By GMU's admission, crunch culture is the most publicised and front-facing problematic by-product within video game development. The organisation also strives to tackle zero-hour and mass temporary contract employment; unsustainable hiring practices and working conditions, lack of severance and proper crediting standards, among several other employee-focused areas.[18]

No one's perfect. Not the media covering video game and mental health matters, not game developers and not gaming studios. Sometimes matters are tackled well and sometimes they are not. While this remains the case, there is room for progress and the opportunity for real, demonstrable change, both in how the industry operates and how it is represented worldwide in terms of its relationship with mental health.

When considering my own mental health journey and the lessons learned I keep finding video games I've loved inextricably entwined with my own experiences and awareness. I've hoped that my video game journalism has tackled mental health with the most sensitivity and compassion as possible, shining a light on a medium that truly has the potential to improve players' lives, should they want them to.

★ ★ ★

Thinking back to that evening my father delivered the news – after my mum had returned from her bedroom, eyes bloodshot, mascara smeared halfway down her face – my parents set off in the car for Portobello, the coastal suburb of Edinburgh where my aunt and uncle lived at the time. I remember wandering around the house on my own, admiring and despising the stillness all at once. I cleaned out the cat's litter tray, which, at 22 years old, was something I don't think I had ever done by my own volition before. I remember the horrible smell from the cat litter nipping my nostrils. I remember a rushing between my ears that sounded like an untuned telly coupled with that irritating hissing noise a radiator bleeder valve makes when expelling air. I collected my girlfriend from her parents' house around the corner. We watched *Beetlejuice* and it was all a bit surreal.

My memories of the next few days are vague. I remember taking time off work and helping out as and where I could. My father and I visited the registrar at Edinburgh City Council headquarters to file my uncle's death, and I remember being taken aback by a phrase on the document: *Cause of death: Ligature strangulation*. Seeing it in writing made it undeniably permanent.

Months later, I visited the block of Portobello flats my uncle had been working on with my mum. Two of the three were finished, and the standard was remarkable, furnished with the sort of décor you might expect in a Spanish villa – spacious and streamlined, real wooden floors, immaculate white walls, sloping windows. The bottom floor flat was a shell, however, mostly due to the fact my uncle couldn't sell the others above amid an increasingly stagnating housing market. When we visited, my mum ushered us around the rooms, inconsequentially pointing out the differences between this building site and the fully-formed works of art above. Before long, we entered the back room, within which a thick, exposed wooden joist ran the width of it, suspended half a foot or so from the ceiling. Mum and I exchanged the briefest of glances, and I knew then, without words, that this was where Jim had taken his own life. The entire time, I wanted nothing more than to batter a *BioShock* Splicer over the head with an oversized virtual spanner.

A NEW CHALLENGER APPEARS

My mental health story is specific to me, just like yours is to you. Parts of our stories might overlap. If you live with, or have lived with depression and anxiety then they probably will. You've probably felt so down that you've struggled to haul yourself out of bed in the morning (it's way worse in winter, right?), or have found yourself back under the covers straight after your working day. You've perhaps felt so anxious that you've bailed on important social engagements, or you've forced yourself along and have drank a shit ton of booze just to function in public. You'll almost certainly have regretted it the next morning, and for the five days thereafter, when that lovely mix of hangover and dark thoughts hits you like a truck and has you second-guessing the most trivial exchanges of last Saturday night that only you care about.

I've had suicidal thoughts but have only once come close to doing anything drastic. And even then, I'm not sure how far I'd have taken it. In my experience of chatting with other people with depression, anxiety and other forms of mental illness, I've noticed their tendency to play down their own circumstances against other experiences. 'I've got it bad, but not as bad as them' isn't an uncommon point of view, yet it's daft. Your story is important – just as important as theirs, regardless of circumstance and specifics. If you're yet to tell yours, I hope that my story inspires you to open up. I hope that, like me, you'll feel better for doing so.

My mental health story is, of course, one story. The popular figure that health departments, services and charities often use is that approximately one in four people experience mental problems every year.[1] While the original 2007 survey that the figure is based on actually says that nearly one person in four (23 per cent) in England, specifically, had at least one psychiatric disorder (and 7.2 per cent had two or more disorders) that year,[2] the message remains that mental health issues have been and can be prevalent. Despite how lost or alone or consumed by that big dark cloud hanging over your head you may feel, you are not alone.

Throughout *Checkpoint*, I want to turn attention to other stories. You're going to know mine quite well by the end so I have widened the perspective of this book by asking others to contribute their own experiences of mental health in conjunction with playing video games in these wee segments called 'A New Challenger Appears'. This phrase is mostly known these days as an internet meme, but it transports me back to the early '90s, playing *Street Fighter 2* with my mates, huddled round a Super Nintendo console and passing the control pads between us.

During the process of writing this book, I interviewed game developers, designers, psychiatrists, entrepreneurs, charities, journalists, community managers and more. You'll be hearing a lot from them throughout, but I also want to showcase the raw mental health stories fully in their own words. The following very personal, very heartfelt accounts that appear between some chapters will offer more insight into the unique tales of game enthusiasts. We will look at how those games are used as coping mechanisms and how they challenge their inner monologues, reach closure, consider things from a different perspective, battle their demons, to balance out and overcome their mental health struggles. Here's our first new challenger:

JOHNNY CHIODINI

Johnny Chiodini is a video game and board game journalist, whose 2016 'Low Batteries' video series explores how mental health is depicted in video games. The series featured on leading video games website Eurogamer — *during which time Johnny was Senior Video Producer — and received critical acclaim from the specialist and mainstream press alike.* Eurogamer's *community hailed the series as informative and ground-breaking, which encouraged the website's readers and viewers to share their own mental health stories with Johnny personally.*

More recently, Johnny's work in promoting video games and mental health awareness led him to be invited to host a TEDx talk in Oldham. Entitled 'Can a Video Game Save a Life?', the talk explores the impact video games can have on mental health and wellbeing and is a must-watch, whether you're interested in video games or not.

"Low Batteries' came to be through sheer fluke, that's the best way I can describe it. I didn't really decide to make the series until the day the first episode went out. I was working on the *Eurogamer* video channel, I knew I had to get a video up that day, but I didn't have anything planned. Everything I was trying was really trite and I hated it because I was feeling really depressed at the time.

'I went for a shower, and I thought to myself, *Okay, I'm feeling awful, so why don't I talk about the fact that I'm feeling awful?* I'd done a feature before on mental health and video games and the games that get mental health right. I was like, *Sod it, why don't I do that again, make a series, I won't tell anyone about it beforehand.* And then I was like, *Oh crap, what am I going to call it?* It sounds really cliché to say it came to me in the shower, but basically, that's what happened. I didn't think too much about it, I simply felt my way through and 'Low Batteries' seemed to just, well, work. It was a serendipitous bit of inspiration off the back of me feeling dreadful.

'Before then, I'd thought idly about exploring mental health, but it was only really after I first sat down and started writing the script for 'Low Batteries' – which was a really cathartic experience itself – that I realised it was something I wanted to keep doing. I thought that if I was using it to explore my own feelings of depression and anxiety, it might be good to try and explore other conditions and disorders, shine a light on them, which was difficult, because I'm not a medical professional and I was concerned about being inadvertently misleading or harmful. Getting that first episode out made me realise it felt right, and in turn, wanted to keep going.

'The feedback at the time was lovely. It felt strange, but the thing that people expressed most was gratitude in that I was using my platform to raise awareness about something they could relate to that not everyone was talking about. In the first few episodes, I related a lot of what I was saying to my own experiences and tried to make it personal without it being solely an account of what life is like for me. I think that helped people relate to it. One of my goals for the series was to cover all bases, to make sure that I always defined my terms when I was talking about something, and make sure I gave as close to the medical definition of a disorder as I was able. Without intending to, it meant that the series was more accessible to people who don't suffer from mental illness.

'I had a few people who told me they'd shown friends and relatives the videos. That was really touching, because one of the most difficult things about mental illness is that it's difficult to articulate how you're feeling at the time and in the moment. The idea that I was able to help people find ways of expressing themselves was unexpected, and that was mind-blowing for me.

'In terms of storytelling, I think it can be hugely cathartic for people playing games to feel like they've done a thing, they've completed a task, or have overcome an obstacle. I'm sure everyone has been pumped up by watching a good action movie, but it's not the same as feeling like *you* did that thing, that you overcame *that* challenge. My scientific knowledge is limited, but, as far as I understand it, achieving something in a video game can give you a release of serotonin, which can in turn, give you a sense of accomplishment that you might be lacking in your day-to-day life. No one has walked away feeling euphoric because they've finished the washing up, but games give you a sense of agency that really empowers the medium to do brilliant things.

'Which is why we find games like *Journey* so beautiful. The tactile sense of wandering around its world and exploring its spaces yourself, I think, is what makes it so profound. If it were an animation, for example, if Pixar had made *Journey*, it would have been very moving – people would be talking about it in the same way people do about the first ten minutes of the animated film *Up* – but it still wouldn't be the same. I think that's what's really interesting. For me, that's also what fuels the negative stories in the tabloids. They're worried that you're playing *Call of Duty,* you're pointing the gun, you're pulling the trigger. So, while they're perfectly happy to talk about James Bond being brilliant and bastion of British culture, the idea that somebody is using a controller to point a gun and pull a trigger themselves, that's what really terrifies them.

'When I'm feeling down, at the moment, Rare's pirate-themed action-adventure game *Sea of Thieves* is the big one I'm playing at the minute. That game for me can be all things, it just depends on what you're looking for. If I'm playing by myself, I'll maybe go fishing, or I might do some quests where I'm looking at a map and digging treasure up. I also have a bunch of friends that I play with online. One of them has a young child, so he can't get out of the house too much. Another one moved away, so instead of meeting up and going to the pub, we'll spend a Friday night, on the Discord online chat app, playing *Sea of Thieves* together, and absolutely roaring around the floor with laughter. Sometimes I can't sleep afterwards, because it's been so much fun. For me, *Sea of Thieves* is a game that can be very quiet, slow and contemplative; but it can also be an absolutely hilarious high-octane form of fun.

'Besides that, I get a lot of use out of my Nintendo Switch, and I play a lot of Motion Twin's *Dead Cells*. There's something about the roguelike genre of video games – where players learn new skills and abilities over the course of the game, used to overcome obstacles and enemies – which I find so fulfilling. When I was a child, I'd always play games on the lowest difficulty setting, which made me feel powerful and capable. The sense of progression you get from them is hard to beat and is something that's really comforting for me.'

CHAPTER 2

SEEKING ASYLUM

HORROR & STEREOTYPES

In January 1991, aged just 63 years old, my maternal grand-mother, Mary, suffered a brain haemorrhage. A subarachnoid haemorrhage, to be specific – an uncommon type caused by bleeding on the surface of the brain. It sounds awful because it is awful. In the six and a bit years that she lived thereafter, her quality of life became so diminished that she required round-the-clock care. She was resigned to a wheelchair, had become incontinent and had lost the ability to speak, all despite extensive surgery in the immediate wake of the stroke. Like many of her generation raised in working-class Glasgow, Mary drank, smoked, and exercised infrequently, impacting factors which doctors reckon contributed to her sickness and narrowed her chances of survival.

She was in and out of the hospital, latterly a nursing home, suffering a string of Transient Ischaemic Attacks (mini strokes) and a number of regular strokes in those six years. 'Are you going to get that?' my granny asked during a visit one evening. A phone rang elsewhere in Glasgow's Southern General Hospital ward. 'Where do you think you are?' my mum replied. In her head, Mary was at home. She was back in Pollok, the area in which she lived in the Southside of Glasgow. She was not on Ward 67.

Vascular cognitive impairment and dementia were conditions mum researched in the medical journals housed in her local library. She learned that these, as well as seizures and strokes were, apparently, common post-brain haemorrhage symptoms. In such circumstances, the patient's comprehension and awareness can and often does deteriorate as a result. She learned this herself because she was never told. In a world pre-Google, pre-smartphones, pre-internet, pre-instantaneous answers at the touch of a button, mum spent hours combing through foreign literature, trying to make sense of what was happening to Mary before putting her findings to medical professionals. The doctors, it turned out, didn't want to worry her with outcomes that may or may not present themselves.

In the summer of 1991, Mary had a massive seizure in our living room. Mum and dad were making food in the kitchen at the time, and I was playing *Sonic the Hedgehog* on the Mega Drive on the big telly. After that, Mary was prescribed an indefinite course of anti-epilepsy medication. Her mobility was grossly affected as the drugs subdued her increasingly restricted movement. In 1995, Mary had another significant stroke and was admitted to full-time care at the advice of her doctors. After searching at length – several visits and dozens of phone calls – my mum chose a nursing home not far from her my granny's house in Pollok. The next two years would see her fade further still as she crept into herself, the illness gradually getting the better of her.

'Your hair is lovely, Mary,' my mum complimented on one visit. 'Who cut it for you?' Mary raised her arm slowly and pointed a finger at herself. At this point, she relied on other people to handle her personal care. Cutting her own hair was out of the question.

By 1997, Mary had stopped speaking altogether. Every Thursday after school I'd be doing my homework while my mum, who was there every night at that point, would engage Mary in a one-way conversation. We'd sit for a few hours before leaving. I still treasure these memories. This characterisation is the only one I have of my granny: one where she sits quietly, vacant, watching mum talk to her in a nursing home and watching me scribble into an A5 jotter.

In March of that year, we lost Mary due to complications from a chest infection. Given her lengthy deterioration to this point, it was a fairly quick and painless way for her to go. Throughout the illness – from her first diagnosis at the hospital and early treatment on the NHS, to the private nursing home care she received at the end – she was well looked after. My granny's conditions wouldn't be considered mental illness per se, but her severe brain trauma distinctly affected her understanding, cognition and, at times, her mood.

★ ★ ★

What does all of this have to do with video games? Representation. Whenever I think of the fine institutional care Mary received in the final stretch of her life, I can't help to compare her experience to the grossly inaccurate and archaic depictions of mental health institutions in popular culture that I see all too often. You probably do too, with or without knowing it. In video games specifically, titles like *Outlast, BioShock Infinite, The Evil Within* and *Asylum* all paint outmoded depictions of mental health institutions, wherein patients are unhinged, violent, and out to harm the protagonist, themselves, or both. These examples were all released in the last ten years, which makes their decision to play into ill-informed, lazy tropes all the more tiresome. Every one of these games could have easily maintained their elsewhere effective atmospheric horror bent without relying on stereotypes.

One harrowingly effective example of horror and mental illness done *right*, however, is LKA's previously mentioned *The Town of Light* – the psychological adventure set inside the Volterra, a long-shuttered mental health institution whose abandoned grounds are still accessible today. You might remember that in the game the player explores the meticulously reconstructed Volterra and relives the history of the main character – a 16 year-old named Renée – through her confused and terrified viewpoint.

LKA's founder and director Luca Dalcò knew of the Volterra as a child but was never fully aware of the asylum within its grounds. In 2012, when visiting the institution as an adult, he was charmed and unsettled by its dark and abandoned pavilions that had been reclaimed by nature around them. I asked Dalcò what it was like to delve into this eerie-sounding world. 'It was like I could breathe the shadow of the past. After that, I started studying the history of mental institutions and I became certain I wanted to make a game about Volterra and what happened there.'

The Town of Light takes a nuanced view of mental health and horror, leveraging realism, facts and history as its means of portraying horror. As such, one of the biggest challenges for Dalcò during development was paying respect and being consistently aware of the sensitive nature of the game's subject matter. Another huge challenge for Dalcò was nailing his research, which took years to undertake. The harrowing nature of the studies he uncovered made the process harder still, and he recalls being overwhelmed with emotion reading about the suffering of particular patients. Renée's character came to life through the very real people Dalcò researched, as he quickly came to the grave realisation that the realities of Volterra were far worse than any perverted fantasy he and his colleagues could conjure in the studio.

'The expulsion these people faced from the society, people who nowadays are considered perfectly normal, is something that hurt me so much,' Dalcò added. 'Then, you could have been locked away in an asylum because you were homosexual, or because a wife didn't want to have sex with her husband, or because you drank too much.'

Dalcò reveals that one of the most unsettling discoveries he made about Volterra, in an operational sense, was the fact that patients were not treated based on diagnosed conditions, but on their behaviours. The institution housed so-called 'tranquil', 'agitated' and 'grimy' wards, and its doctors and nurses sought to control their patients like livestock. Opened in 1888 and shuttered in 1978, Dalcò explains that medicine for mental health conditions were non-existent. The fact that hundreds of patients were assigned to single doctors working excruciating hours, so scant were resources, only lowered the standard of care across the board. It wasn't unusual for patients to be tied and bound to prevent them harming themselves or others, and that the use of 'experimental' treatments – such as electrocon-vulsive therapy – to reduce the symptoms of schizophrenia and depression were common practice.

'By modern standards, these methods were simply torture. It was also normal to destroy part of the brain to stop those poor people suffering so much. We must not forget that the culture at that time was that a "mad" person was not a proper person, which was a fact that almost everyone accepted.'

One person who did not accept this idea was Angelo Lippi, the former head of social services at the Italian psychiatric hospital, Zona Alta Val di Cecina, who LKA consulted with during *The Town of Light's* development. I spoke to Lippi after the game's console launch in 2016, because, while Dalcò's immaculate research and inspirations for making the game itself proved invaluable insights, this was someone who once worked in the vicinity of Volterra, in operation and at ground level.

'I was not surprised when the asylums were closed. From my first day on the job, I always felt that asylums were not the proper place to ensure adequate care that could help patients to return to their lives.'

Situated in a quaint mountaintop town in the Tuscany region of Italy, the Zona Alta Val di Cecina was once part of Volterra. According to Lippi, the institution was dubbed by locals as 'the place of no return', on account of the fact the patients were often institutionalised indefinitely. In institutions like this, patients were subjected to archaic treatments, such as prolonged isolation; trephination, where small parts of the skull are removed using an auger, bore or saw; and bloodletting and purging, whereby blood and vomit was forcefully drawn from the patient as a perceived means of restoring internal imbalances. Between 1970 and 2003, Lippi worked in the adjacent Zona Alta Val di Cecina in a social work role that was then still finding its place in society, particularly within the realms of psychiatric care.

'Finding solutions for therapy and inclusion in society, and family life for those who had 'real' mental illness, could be envisaged,' she continued. 'I was pleased and proud to have worked in Volterra, and with its director Carmelo Pellicanò in particular, who led these great battles for innovation.'

From a video game development perspective, Dalcò insists that an unwavering desire to do a horrible topic justice combined with aspirations of doing something different drove much of *The Town of Light's* creation. Jump scares and cheap stereotypes are all well and good but they won't stick with you hours, weeks, even years after playing – something which has been directly reflected in the feedback LKA has received since its launch.

'Our feedback has easily been the most rewarding part of the whole experience,' adds Dalcò. 'We have also received negative reviews, of course, but it doesn't hurt because those are usually from people that would expect jump scares and so on. Most of the people appreciated the game in a deeply touching way.

'I also put a lot of me into *The Town of Light*, through my own experiences and feelings. I felt exposed when the game was released. It was great to feel people understand and get emotionally involved. That was truly great, it really was, and is something I don't know if I'll have the chance to experience ever again.'

Echoing the sentiments of Dalcò, LKA environmental artist Lorenzo Conticelli explains to me that he was determined to tell the story of Volterra as soon as he saw the abandoned building in person. Like Dalcò, he and the rest of the developer's team became increasingly adamant that their story would not pull any punches. It would tell the graphic, often gruesome truth about Volterra and psychiatric institutions in general at that time.

'No one knows the story of this place, and we wanted to tell it. During our research we found these controversial, dark and sad topics and we didn't want to hide anything from the player. We decided to show everything that we found in our research. I feel this is the only way to approach these controversial topics if you want to do them justice: treat them with respect and sensitivity and tell the truth of what happened.'

Through the experiences of Renée, *The Town of Light* serves to tell Volterra's horrid truths as they occurred in reality. Under flashbacks driven by diary entries strewn around the institution's lonely corridors, examination rooms and isolation chambers, players uncover Renée's journey as a 16-year-old girl who, in 1938, was institutionalised. She spends much of her life held against her will, while continuously clashing with orderlies, nurses and doctors, both mentally and physically. She is seen being forcibly given electroshock therapy, which Conticelli tells me was researched by watching live videos of inpatients going through the same barbaric procedure. In another scene, the player is made to witness Renée being raped. It's in these moments where the true horror of the institution is made real for the player.

Further bucking the tropes of horror, unlike the vast majority of horror games take place beneath the cover of darkness, *The Town of Light* is set in the afternoon, where huge Victorian windows spread blankets of sunlight across the institute's cobweb-covered floors.

'The whole game uses light as a metaphor,' Conticelli elaborates. 'You can hide in the dark, but you can't hide in the light, you can't escape the light. The title and storyline for *The Town of Light* came from the diary of a schizophrenic girl who remembered, in an altered state, that she saw this brilliant bright light that filled her mind. We tried to create this contrast – from the outside it seems like a normal day, then you take this journey inside which is at times really dark. I think the environment and the structure helps to keep the dark inside.

'When the script was finished, Luca met some with some psychologists, psychiatrists, and social workers, to get their opinions. They all assured him *The Town of Light* was close to how it was. They gave him more background information, too – such as the smells inside the asylum.'

While we're yet to have reached a future where in-game smells are expelled via our consoles, all this information gathered by the LKA team is unmistakably present during a playthrough. You can feel the light's warmth between the shadows and smell the damp in the heavy air.

Balancing this with the game's darkest moments made for some gruelling development sessions, particularly at junctures where the team transferred video research into working in-game set pieces. Still, Conticelli remains firmly of the view that, even with the difficulties that go into creating something of this nature, there is no better medium like video games to tell a story as heartfelt and sobering.

'Using video games to tell these stories is really important because, when playing, you are not passive. In *The Town of Light*, your decisions are based on how you explore the asylum. Games are amazing for encouraging choices based on players' motivations and can help them internalise the messages better than any other medium.'

* * *

'The oldest and strongest emotion of mankind is fear, and the oldest and strongest kind of fear is fear of the unknown,' reads the opening line of HP Lovecraft's perennial 1927 essay 'Supernatural Horror in Literature'. The idea of fear deriving from unfamiliar circumstance long predates the esteemed horror fiction author's slant on terror, and is a view still held by many today – which is fine up to a point. It's fine until it bleeds into other more ambiguous areas, such as mental illness. Perhaps perpetuated by the archaic institutions that once served the mentally ill, this notion of viewing mental health through the lens of 'the unknown', and thus as something that's to be feared, only serves to bolster the tired tropes which, in the 21st century, we should really have moved on from by now.

But it's not all doom and gloom. Many have challenged video games' generalised interpretation of mental illness, and that games have an onus to be more responsible for their depictions. I couldn't agree more, and neither could Asylum Jam's Lucy Morris.

Asylum Jam was a personal mission for Morris after losing her step-sister to suicide, having watched partners and friends deal with similar difficulties and her own complex experiences with grief following the sudden passing of her mother. A very general overarching realisation from participants of the jam is that it takes creative design to successfully pull off, but creating horror video games that don't feed into harmful tropes isn't too difficult at all. Through this process, one message that's important to preserve is that while video game developers can and should do more to sidestep stereotypes, mental illness *is* scary, especially for the first time. No matter the wealth of research that exists today, from an individual's perspective, it is the overwhelming 'unknown' that is feared. It shouldn't be feared *because* it's the unknown, but because we all tend to fear what we're unfamiliar with. The most important thing to consider here when considering a very personal fear is *how* this fear is portrayed in any medium – how it's done in terms of themes, concept and rhetoric.

While there's been a degree of ongoing critical thought into the representation of mental illness and the horror genre of video games, using sanity as a mechanic or antipathic patients as antagonists are trends that have far from vanished. *Outlast* is a first-person survival horror game created by a developer Red Barrels in 2013. Its frantic take on cat-and-mouse survival is undeniably enjoyable but its poor portrayal of mental illness and its reliance on clichés is its significant downfall. It is set in a decrepit, draughty asylum where patients are deranged and exist to be the player's enemy. The writing, concerning progressive mental health discussions, is archaic. During my years writing about video games, I asked to interview Red Barrels about these topics several times but was (politely) declined on every occasion.

Morris believes that beyond these pitfalls, *Outlast* is incredibly well done in its execution. While she strongly disagrees with censorship – 'creative expression is always going to be subjective' – she is of the view that the game, and many others like it, didn't need to rely on these narrative tropes, already being a well-orchestrated, terrifying thrill-ride packed with jump scares.

'When game designing, it's very easy to fall into tropes and imitate past successes,' says Morris. 'For instance, a large amount of cosmic horror is based on using "sanity" as a depletable resource because that's simply how it's been interpreted for a long period of time – for example, games like *Amnesia: The Dark Descent* and *Elder Sign*.'

Depletable resources have often been the bedrock of game-design: this is where a player will either be given or will have to gain, a finite amount of an essential life-preserving source which can appear under a range of names but generally surmount to energy, stamina, hunger, health and, crucially, life. In *The Legend of Zelda* series, protagonist Link's three hearts are a depletable source – when he's out of hearts, he's out of life and it's game over. In *Amnesia: The Dark Descent*, when you run out of the sanity resource, you become, simply, insane.

'There are definitely ways to think about how we can differently interpret resources that may both open up new design avenues to excite players, and more respectfully treat mental illness.

'I think to some degree, unfortunately, tropes will always exist. They're shorthand and immediately relatable and used for such reasons. That said, I do think we can perhaps make them less common or create better, positive stereotypes. At the very least, creators are talking about these mechanics more and having discussions about them during the design stage. Awareness is really important and problematic matters aren't thought of as an actual issue without being invited to a discussion about it. We just need to keep talking and encouraging positive creativity.'

Morris believes that growing, changing and evolving the

discussion around mental health is a complicated process, and while she endeavours to talk about her own mental health in public forums in a bid to help normalise the conversation, she well-understands the personal and idiosyncratic nature of mental health, and why others might not be so forthcoming.

'I think having more pop culture content approaching it in a healthy, conversational way would be really good; normalising these discussions with our friends and family, and being supportive. It's a big challenge and I'm not sure there is one right answer to it. I'm not a health professional, so anything I say should be taken with a grain of salt but from my own perspective there's still a certain societal taboo about discussing mental health and associated topics. Horror and social discomfort are often brought about by the unknown and things we don't understand – and it's easy to demonise something when you're not educated about its nature.

'I think video games are equally accountable – sure, they have an extra element of interactivity, but they're a medium just like literature and film, who are also not innocent in this debate. They borrow from each other in an ecosystem, and as each medium will influence someone in a different way, we need to think about the specific responsibilities of each medium when we create.'

Morris describes the aforementioned *Town of Light* as a 'super important' contribution to the ongoing discussion of mental health in games, and names Killbite Studio's *Among The Sleep* – a first-person exploration game seen through the eyes of a toddler – as her go-to recommendation.

With each passing year, Asylum Jam grows beyond Morris'

wildest expectations and, while delighted with the flow of personal testimonials and stories she's received since day one, she now wonders if the game jam has made its point. Morris will always be proud of what she and her partners achieved, but she carries that positive ethos forward in her work at the indie studio Starcolt.

'I've always been an avid reader and I love literature, but I've always connected with games on a different and more intense emotional level. You can create entire physical worlds out of nothing, weave interactive stories however you want, fall in love or absolutely hate characters you pull out of nowhere. Games are quite magical in an interactive sense and have a lot of power to absorb players in more ways than just mechanical enjoyment. It's such an exciting creative profession to be part of, and I'm always so blown away by what we create.'

★ ★ ★

When talking about the intersections of horror and mental illness, I would be remiss to leave out the refreshing example of Polish developer Super Sexy Software (SSS)'s *The Shattering*. It tells the story of John Evans, an everyman who suffers from depression, bipolar disorder and psychosis as a result of traumatic events experienced in his past. The idea driving John's character is that his story is relatable and that all players will be able to find something in common with him and his thought process. To ensure this was handled in a sensitive and constructive manner, SSS consulted with a professional psychiatrist who drew up a character profile for protagonist John Evans. CEO Marta Szymańska knew that mental health professionals had to be consulted from the conception of the idea for *The Shattering*.

'Firstly, like most projects, we did a lot of reading, getting into it, understanding the subject, and there are some issues that we weren't sure if we could handle correctly. This game is scientifically based but is nevertheless going to be a game. We visited the doctor who helped us create John as if he was real. We were also encouraged to focus on how people act, how people talk, how you should talk to them, how to interact with them, how to suggest things, how to suggest direction – and that all helped us to build the game.'

The Shattering showed me that this was a game unafraid to break the status quo and gave me optimism. For SSS, mental health was not going to be a thoughtless gore-fest. Fear of the unknown is central to its delivery of horror, but in a self-reflective manner. Its terror thrives in a combination of John's circumstances and how they may or may not relate to the player. It's a difficult line to walk; but here is proof it can be done and done well.

'*The Shattering* looks at the shattering mind, what the protagonist doesn't want to remember,' Szymańska concludes during our chat. 'And why doesn't he want to remember? Because he's been through traumatic events. So, what happened in his life? We put everything together and focused on mental illness because everyone today could have it, and I think that's the horror aspect of this game: if you have depression, if you feel sad, you know emotions yourself. If you can see it through and understand John, in such a way, I think that'll push players towards eventually acknowledging those emotions. Mental illness fits here naturally, somehow.'

CHAPTER 3

ONE LIFE LEFT

PERMADEATH & SUICIDE

'll cut to the chase: sometimes, life is awful. If I've learned nothing else it's that we're at the mercy of misfortune and that depression does not discriminate. That's the reality, and as clichéd as it sounds, we must roll with the lows in order to appreciate the highs. Uncle Jim's lows ran deeper than most, to the point where, in his eyes, they became insurmountable.

My mum's favourite film is Frank Capra's 1946 drama *It's a Wonderful Life*, which, given its content, feels like another cruel twist of irony. There's an alcove at the far end of her living room, where, for as long as I can remember, a theatrical release poster of the Christmas fantasy hangs. The image portrays George Bailey (played by James Stewart) lifting Mary Hatch (Donna Reed) by her waist over his head as the two-beam pristine white smiles back at one another. The plot of *It's a Wonderful Life*, however, paints a darker tale. If you're not familiar with it (I never begrudge anyone for not knowing the classics, life's too short), ~~after getting himself into financial bother,~~ George Bailey plans his suicide on Christmas Eve, 1945. A guardian angel, Clarence Odbody (Henry Travers), responds to George's family's prayers when they sense that something is off, who in turn, stops George from throwing himself off of a bridge. Instead, Clarence takes George on a Charles Dickens-esque journey that imagines life in Bedford Falls, sans the protagonist. George then decides not to kill himself, manages to overcome his financial woes, and everyone lives happily ever after.

Given that the property my uncle had struggled to sell prior to his death sold just weeks after his passing (which would have cleared his debt), some uncomfortable parallels can be drawn between Frank Capra's drama and Jim's situation. My uncle was, by and large, a private man, and as such we as a family sadly didn't sense that something was off. I'm nevertheless convinced that had he felt able to chat about his circumstances, he'd still be here today. Which is, in essence, what George Bailey was forcefully given – an ear to bend. Depictions of guardian angels and 'what if' scenarios are fantastical, but by being shown how the people in his life would cope without his influence, George realises that money is not the most important thing in the world, and that he's got so much to live for.

Author and mental health advocate Kevin Hines explores a real-world variation of this tale in his award-winning 2013 memoir *Cracked, Not Broken* where he details the extreme and instant regret he felt milliseconds after jumping from the Golden Gate Bridge several years ago. He tells of how, after surviving the 220ft drop, he wanted to not only live his life, but raise awareness around mental illness and deter others who might be in a similar situation to the one he was in once.

After watching *It's a Wonderful Life* afresh several years after Jim's death, and subsequently reading Hines' book, I inevitably thought about how permanence is explored in video games; a medium for which new starts and do-overs are one of its unique selling points. I considered how video games explore autonomy and what the consequences of dying can possibly be in a virtual world. After all, to paraphrase *Neverending Nightmares* developer Matt Gilgenbach, we assume a degree of agency when handling virtual death; we refer to *ourselves* as having died, not the characters we control. In video games that utilise perma-death – permanent death: a feature whereby singular death is final, where dying means starting a game again from square one without continues or extra lives – more significance is placed on the loss of life. As a result of the subgenre's increasing popularity in recent years, Dictionary.com introduced the word 'permadeath' as it relates to video games in 2015.

The rise of permadeath in video games has changed the way many players approach them. In games where the perma-death mechanic is utilised, emotion drives decision making and mental state often governs players' actions, not logic or rationale. In short, permadeath forces players to consider consequence and finality.

My main question is: are these themes and ideas transferable to reality? If the idea of imposing real-world rules on video games makes them more realistic, can playing those games broaden our interpretation of permanence in reality?

The idea that engaging in certain virtual behaviours has scope to elicit feelings of guilt, which can in turn encourage pro-social, real-life consequences is explored in the article *Being Bad in a Video Game Can Make Us More Morally Sensitive* (Grizzard, Tamborini, Lewis, Wang, Prabhu, 2014). Matthew Grizzard, of the Ohio Stat's University School of Communication, hypothesises that committing immoral behaviours in video games can lead to increased moral sensitivity and a heightened sense of consequence in players. To this end, is it feasible for this line of understanding to allow a better comprehension of suicide – both in-game and in real life?

'I think the question really has two parts,' Dr Grizzard begins. 'One: do video games encourage a better understanding of the finality of suicide in real life? Versus, two: could video games encourage a better understanding of the finality of suicide in real life?

'I don't think games necessarily encourage ideas of permanence and finality. Video games are mostly designed to be played multiple times with death being a temporary inconvenience rather than permanent. Players will sometimes even kill themselves in games when they encounter obstacles or become stuck to respawn at an earlier time point. So video games, particularly popular press video games, encourage a view that death is temporary. Death is portrayed as detrimental in games, but it is not a one-way door.

'I do think games *could* encourage a better understanding of the finality of suicide. Evolutionarily, play represents a safe place to practice or experience skills that we generally don't or can't have direct access to in the real world for many reasons – for safety reasons, ethical reasons, that sort of thing. Both predatory and prey animals play to learn how to survive in the wild. Human play serves similar roles, with the skills that we learn being not only related to physical attributes but also social attributes.

'For example, in medical schools in the US, doctors in training practice giving bad news to patients in "play" scenarios with actors. These scenarios help doctors practice skills that they rarely have the opportunity to practice in the real world in a safe environment where making mistakes has few consequences. Video games can be particularly adept at allowing the same type of play for several reasons. Primarily, the human brain doesn't firmly distinguish between real-versus-mediated stimuli. Our brain similarly reacts to mediated images as it does to real images. This is why scary movies can make us jump or tearjerkers can make us cry.'

Dr Grizzard further elaborates on how video games fit into this instinctual empathy using coincidental comparison that hits close to home.

'Video games have the potential to provide players with a rich virtual environment filled characters and stimuli that they respond to as if they were real. As such, games could provide a glimpse into the severe negative consequences of suicide on family members and friends, in a fashion similar to the classic American film *It's a Wonderful Life*. This glimpse is obviously impossible in the real world, but games have the ability to simulate it.'

Maybe my mum's favourite film was years ahead of its time, a glimpse into how second chances are not only a moving method of storytelling but a potential mechanic within the origins of yarn-spinning itself.

The relative youthfulness of the video games medium means there is less academic research available relating to games compared to more traditional media. That said, with game consoles, PCs, tablets, smartphones and handhelds, access to video games is more prevalent today than it has ever been.

With everything Dr Grizzard poses in mind, here is a list of permadeath video games worthy of your time, including those that made me consider finality beyond their virtual bounds.

★ ★ ★

THE LONG DARK
Developer: Hinterland Studio
Genre: Exploration/Survival
Year of release: 2017

'No hand-holding' is the tagline used in the promotional material of Hinterland Studio's exploration/survival game *The Long Dark*, and, wow, does it follow through on that sentiment. In the game's Survival Mode, players are dropped into a gorgeous snow-swept 50 square kilometre playing area in the Northern Canadian wilderness, in a world recovering from a massive geomagnetic anomaly. Ultimately, all modern technology has been rendered obsolete, and each life lived in this world is randomised with every playthrough. This means that each expedition is different from the last – buildings, supplies, landmarks, water sources, among other key locations, never feature in the same place twice, making all playthroughs unique.

Upon death, your save file is deleted and gone forever and in the absence of a direct narrative, your central goal is to survive. You're tasked with scouring the landscape for supplies as you monitor your hunger, thirst, fatigue and temperature, balancing your gathered resources as you go. You hunt and fish, climb and trap, plunder and survive – all the while avoiding hypothermia, frostbite and other life-threatening ailments.

In my most memorable journey, I set up camp in a derelict cabin situated in the centre of a frozen lake. I restored my new dwelling by laying sleeping mats and boarding up the holes in its exterior. I created a fishing hole by drilling the ice outside and gathered firewood to keep myself warm through the night. On one supply excursion, I was surrounded by wolves and, had it not been for my makeshift hand-crafted bow and stone-headed arrows, I'd have been a goner. Upon discovering a hunting rifle on one trip, I took up deer hunting, but nearly shit myself – both in-game and in reality – when I was chased from the woods by a ravenous bear.

After 198 in-game days surviving the wilderness, my longest ever foray into *The Long Dark's* brutal universe, doom struck. In the most underwhelming way. Not at the hands of bears, wolves, deer, or the elements – but from a container of stagnant water, which led to dysentery, and then my untimely death. Rest in peace me. I don't want to know what my headstone would have said. With time moving 12 times quicker in-game than in reality, my almost 200-day venture equated to 16 and a half hours of real-world game time. Despite the monotony of surviving *The Long Dark's* world hour-to-hour, there was something immensely satisfying about the routine I'd carved within its beautiful landscape. So much so, that I've since struggled to recapture the magic of my isolated ice lake shack surrounded by woodland venture.

Upon losing my avatar in this instance, I felt genuine remorse. I wasn't upset to the point of crying, but I was gutted. I'd committed so much of myself to this journey – my wits, my intuition, my time – over a period of months. And now it was gone, forever. I've returned to *The Long Dark* many times since but have failed to recapture the magic of that wonderful 198 day playthrough, and I'm not sure I ever will.

SPELUNKY
Developer: Mossmouth
Genre: Platfomer
Year of release: 2013

Unlike other permadeath video games, survival in *Spelunky* rarely involves luck. So small is its safety net, in fact, that understanding permanence in Mossmouth's platformer is almost exclusively tied to skill and, as I've learned time and time again, frustration.

Like *The Long Dark* and many other permadeath video games, *Spelunky's* worlds are randomly generated, meaning each journey is different from the last and the next in turn. In search of treasure, you're sent deep underground to explore a series of caverns, caves, craters and chasms, all brimming with monsters, traps and shotgun-wielding shopkeepers. Double cross the latter at your peril.

On the face of it, *Spelunky* is a firm but fair platformer, but as you play, as you learn its quirks and its idiosyncrasies, it becomes more than that. It's precisely engineered. It's a test of mettle, of hand-to-eye coordination, of reflexes and reaction times. It made me contemplate risk-versus-reward like no other video game. It kept me guessing, its randomness threw curveballs at me, it charmed me with its cast of silent characters who, after hours and hours of misadventure, I felt closer to than some people I've met in person. Death in *Spelunky* is obsessive, because each failed attempt is a result of your own missteps, and very rarely down to luck or chance. In *Spelunky,* the margin for error is so small, as in real life.

HOLLOW KNIGHT

Developer: Team Cherry
Genre: Action/Adventure
Year of release: 2017

Team Cherry's *Hollow Knight* is a gorgeous 2D side-scrolling action role-playing game, which, like *Spelunky*, sends players into a vast, interconnected world of ruined cities, lost highways, turgid swamps and thick jungles. Named Hallownest, the game's nightmarish playground can be explored in whichever order the player desires, which lends it a fluidity rarely found in games of this kind. This degree of agency places greater onus on decision making, and underscores the fact that every in-game action levies its own set of consequences – be that while fighting each of the game's 130 enemies and 30 bosses, or while setting off to discover untravelled pockets of its sprawling underworld. Upon completing *Hollow Knight* the first time round, a new game mode named Steel Soul Mode is unlocked, offering players the 'ultimate challenge', which is, in essence, permadeath.

This changes the complexion of *Hollow Knight* entirely, because suddenly you can no longer rely on continues and check points – both of which I myself leaned upon heavily during my first playthrough. By leveraging routine against me, *Hollow Knight's* Steel Soul mode made me reconsider every bad habit I'd picked up to this point, both combat and exploration, and made me appreciate permanence and finality in a game I thought I'd otherwise figured out.

When I tried to re-enter a failed Steel Soul run, I was asked if I wanted to clear the save slot. Where save slots in previous games told me the location I'd last visited before death, new save slots in Steel Soul Mode were simply identified with the word 'DEFEATED'. Seeing this in writing made death in *Hollow Knight* even more onerous than before.

DARKEST DUNGEON

Developer: Red Hook Studios
Genre: Turn-based Role-playing
Year of release: 2016

Darkest Dungeon utilises traits from all three of the games noted previously, while also folding elements of mental health into its turn-based role-playing game. Designed to consider the stresses of adventuring, players recruit, train and direct a team of flawed heroes inside a gothic world of crypts and warrens filled with monsters and foes. Central to all of this is *Darkest Dungeon's* Affliction system, wherein an in-game stress gauge forces players to consider their warriors' paranoia, fear, irrationality and masochism levels, lest they exhaust themselves on the battlefield. Success, then, is hinged upon how you best mix and match your armies of four. Even a well-trained, well-equipped and well-provisioned team can be struck down in an instant, permanently.

'And when they die, they stay dead,' delivers the game's narrator, someone you'll become intimately acquainted with. Even a seasoned squad – one which has survived four or five or six dungeon runs – can, and will, succumb to *Darkest Dungeon's* most lethal enemy: stress.

Enemy attacks cause stress. Watching a comrade suffer a blow causes stress. Darkness causes stress. Too much light causes stress. Hunger causes stress. Bleeding causes stress. As is consistent with reality: just about anything causes stress. While a full stress bar can have positive effects – such as forcing a permanent agro-state on characters, which make their attacks more powerful – afflictions will more often force maladies upon your squad such as paranoia, masochism and antagonism. Perhaps the afflicted will mock teammates for their lack of valour in battle, which in turn causes the recipient's stress to rise. Maybe they'll retreat in action for fear of a teammate's betrayal. Or maybe they'll flat out refuse to cooperate, even when offered food or remedies if they should wind up on death's door. If any given fighter's stress bar fills a second time, they'll suffer a heart attack on the spot.

'And when they die, they stay dead.'

So, to avoid untimely deaths, de-stressing your mercenaries by way of the hamlet's services becomes not only a necessity but also part of the game's grand strategy. I sent one of my earliest recruits – Dismas, a Highwayman who I'd become particularly fond of early on for, well, not dying immediately – to recover from one notably arduous dungeon run in the town's tavern. Booze, I thought, *that works for me, it'll surely work for him.* In the meantime, I took on some new blood, went about training her up, and completely forgot about my pal Dismas as he searched for restitution at the bottom of the bottle.

In-game weeks passed, comrades came and went, and by the time I realised I'd misplaced my one-time stalwart, I had a paranoid alcoholic on my hands who refused to turn up to work unless heavily inebriated. Through some warped sense of loyalty, I drafted him into the next expedition, where he died a slow and gruelling death. Maybe I should've sent him to the brothel to relieve himself, or to seek penance at the abbey instead? I felt bad but at the same time a sense of relief.

FORTNITE BATTLE ROYALE

Developer: Epic Games
Genre: Battle Royale
Year of release: 2017

Born from its runaway hit predecessor *Fortnite Save the World*, *Battle Royale* is a variation on a theme that drops 100 players into an ever-shortening sandbox map, and has them fighting to the death. The game has evolved beyond recognition since its arrival with new themes, events and sponsored crossovers, but, ultimately, players fight until the last person stands, and once you're out, you're out for good.

Permadeath is used less stringently here, simply because dying and restarting a new game is such a streamlined process. *Fortnite's* enduring popularity means there are millions of full-lobbied games ready to go, so exiting one and entering another takes just minutes. Yet, getting down to the final stretch of combatants can and does make permadeath in each game relevant. Risk versus reward becomes increasingly important as the scores of each game's opponents whittle down, and the playing area around you shortens. Do you find a suitable hiding place and let the remaining fighters battle it out, before swooping in for a last-gasp kill? Do you mark your territory with aggression from beginning to end? Player agency plays a huge part in *Fortnite's* flee or fight mechanics, mixing life and death with quick-fire, real-time decision making.

DARK SOULS

Developer: From Software
Genre: Action Role-playing
Year of release: 2012

Speaking of risk versus reward, few that strike this balance quite like *Dark Souls*. Its take on permadeath is an ambiguous one, in that dying is not wholly permanent, but it can result in losing a key resource – souls – should you take the wrong steps after coming a cropper.

Unlike the majority of modern video games which incorporate autosave systems – a series of automatic safety nets, where failure becomes irrelevant – the *Dark Souls* series incorporates bonfire checkpoints. Souls are farmed from fallen enemies and act as the currency that facilitates progression. Levelling up can only be done at a bonfire. Once killed, you lose whatever souls you were carrying and they can only be redeemed in the immediate next life. This means trekking from the last bonfire you rested at to wherever you were struck down, marked by a pool of your previous body's blood. If you die again before recovering the souls of the previous turn, they're gone for good.

All of which poses two questions: Do you play it safe and slouch between each bonfire, gripping the smattering of souls you've gathered with both hands? Or do you wade in, gung-ho, in a bid to snaffle as many lovely souls as you can, all the while running the risk of losing them all? Another conundrum, and another glimpse of permanence and reality seen through risk-versus-reward.

DON'T STARVE

Developer: Klei Entertainment
Genre: Survival
Year of release: 2013

Don't Starve is another game that boasts no hand-holding in its developer blurb, and takes the sentiment to heart. An uncompromising wilderness survival game that riffs on science and magic, *Don't Starve* has players filling the shoes of Wilson, an intrepid scientist, who has been trapped by an otherworldly being in a sprawling wilderness, and who must conquer his new surroundings to survive.

Like most survival games, Wilson starts with nothing to his name, so it's on you to craft, hunt, research, farm, fight and survive on his behalf. Like most of the games previously explored, *Don't Starve* is also powered by randomly generated maps, which makes each playthrough unique. Similar to *Darkest Dungeon,* the grief that follows losing any given Wilson incarnation will be reflected in how long you've managed to keep him alive. My own longest journey lasted 49 in-game days and I was devastated to see Wilson go. A cursory glance at the footage from other players' similarly demoralising ends in *Don't Starve* on YouTube (otherwise known as 'let's plays' where players post anything from highlights of their gameplay to full-on several hour-long videos of their adventures) show some players running past the several *thousand* in-game day mark.

'As designers, we work really hard to give players agency,' Klei Entertainment founder Jamie Cheng explains. 'Permadeath is almost free agency, in that suddenly every action matters a whole lot more. I think players appreciate that, and as a designer it gives us a chance to show them similar scenarios over time, and how their actions can drastically change outcomes.'

'Obviously, emotion plays a part, but in my experience the emotion happens after the finality, not before. When the player dies of a catastrophic event happens – that's when the weight of consciousness hits. Beforehand, players are simply more attuned to their actions and less frivolous.'

Although Cheng admits suicide wasn't necessarily something that was actively considered during *Don't Starve's* design process, he does point to the fact that it's more important to consider the active adventure, as opposed to its end.

'Instead of affecting how players perceive reality, our goal is the other way around – to have a video game that mimics reality in its finality and consequence. In addition, we want players to enjoy the journey. Since the player knows that eventually they'll lose it all, it makes more sense that the process is the interesting part, and not what you get at the end of their journey.'

It could be argued that no matter which way around these ideas are depicted, the result illustrates an intrinsic link between game worlds and the real world. There are of course loads of other video games which explore similar territory. Subset Games' *FTL: Faster Than Light*, is a complex strategy game set in outer space, wherein the constant threat of death adds tension and weight to every action. Firaxis' *XCOM: Enemy Unknown* and its sequel *XCOM 2's* slant on permadeath is similar to that of *Darkest Dungeon*, in that losing any one of your best-trained soldiers out on the intergalactic battleground can feel like a death in the family.

Even *Minecraft*, one of the most popular and most played video games of all time has a Hardcore mode that implements permadeath. Phil Watson (known by Philza on Twitch), is a fine example when he made international news in April 2019 after his five year-long playthrough in the ultra-challenging setting came to an underwhelming end, as four otherwise conquerable enemies cornered him at once. Thwarted by bad luck, Watson later explained on a BBC News television segment that he'd become accustomed to streaming his *Minecraft* game to a modest audience, until his death stream had gone viral, having since been viewed millions of times. Watson spoke of feeling depressed after his permadeath save file was wiped because, after all, he'd committed five years of his leisure time to that point invested in this one particular virtual world.

Perhaps the most striking thing of all in Watson's case, with permanence and finality in mind, is that despite having become an expert *Minecraft* player, his most prized adventure was undone by bad luck – a cruel mix of timing, circumstance and the game's randomly generated monster spawns. Upon death in-game, Watson's grief in real life is palpable, again under-scoring the power of video games to incur emotive response via persuasion and interactivity.

To this end, Dr Grizzard believes video games possess the power to have players relate to their virtual characters as they would real people. However, he again highlights the relative infancy of the gaming medium, therefore the lack of academic study, and subsequently the difficulty in proving any of this conclusively.

'Video games do have the potential to influence players in meaningful ways. However, questions still remain as to whether a single-play experience that associates strong consequences with suicide could overcome the more traditional "death is temporary" play experiences that are generally seen in video games. These are fascinating questions, and I would be hesitant to conclude one way or the other. As always, more research must be done.'

And such research will, and arguably must, continue. What must also continue is the dialogue around mental health: poor mental health and mental illness is not a failure or weakness. I want to echo the statistic about my home country from the opening paragraph of chapter one, because it's one worth repeating: in Scotland, two people kill themselves every single day. Jim became one of those people. Those who knew him mourned the passing of family member and friend. To those who didn't, he became a cruel statistic, and an indictment on our scope as Scottish people to share and talk through our problems. Video games can't single-handedly drive these statistics down, but if specific games can help us to appreciate the finality and permanence of death, if they can offer even the briefest respite for someone to think more about what comes after a decision that would have weighed so heavily on them, then that is a good thing. Video games can't stop suicide, but if they can contribute even slightly towards more open and enlightened conversations around the issue that could help just one person, then that's something to be hopeful about.

CHAPTER 4

SOBERING EXPERIENCES

PUZZLES & ADDICTION

'The demon drink,' said the police officer at the desk, raising a wry smile as he handed back my belongings.

Trainers, belt, phone, keys, wallet, a handful of loose coins. I bowed my head to nod but couldn't bring myself to catch his gaze. I was mortified. I shuffled out of the building, glanced at my watch – 9.32am – and turned towards the hill outside the station. The glare of the Monday morning sunlight made me wince as I headed for my parents' house. I upped my pace to a fast walk, my brow already slick with sweat. I was late for work, and in the meantime had to piece together the previous evening.

* * *

When Jim hanged himself, I was in my early 20s and, like everyone around me at the time, lived my life weekend to weekend. Booze and recreational drugs in Glasgow nightclubs blazed a trail through my formative years via the Sub Club, the Art School, the Garage, and, when they still existed, Archaos, Destiny and the Arches nightclub. Midweek, I worked a labour-intensive job as a plumber, first as an apprentice and then as a fully qualified tradesman, and for the most part, did so to fund my twilight debauchery. In turn, I spent Mondays at work hungover, Tuesdays depressed and Wednesdays subdued. By Thursday I was over the worst of it, and by Friday I was ready to do it all over again. I lived this merry-go-round for several years, my routine occasionally interrupted by 'holidays' to Ibiza, wherein my weekend schedule on home soil became round-the-clock abroad.

If you've ever experienced loss in adulthood, you'll appreciate the importance of reflection. The hows and whys of death were never something 11-year-old me thought twice about when my granny passed in 1997, or when my great aunt left us a few years later. But as an adult, 'what if' was central to my grieving process – a question compounded by the brutal fashion in which Jim ended things. *What if* he'd been able to speak out about how he was feeling? *What if* one of us had seen it coming? *What if* we could turn back time… could any of it have been avoided? The cruellest thing about suicide, from the perspective of those left behind, is that these questions persist but cannot be answered.

Jim was my mother's only brother and last remaining immediate family member. Her mum and dad, my granny, and granda died prematurely – Mary of a brain haemorrhage at 69 and Jimmy of a heart attack at just 42 – while Jim had just turned 53. Behind the tears and her own emotional red wine-inspired salutations, I cannot imagine the pain she felt, and probably still feels, towards the ordeal. I, on the other hand, became obsessed with the nature of Jim's death. Although I wasn't there when he died, I morbidly pictured how he might have looked immediately afterwards – his eyes bulging, face purple, body motionless. I thought about him scrambling around in the days and hours and minutes prior, the weight on the world on his shoulders, frantic, his blood heavy with prescription Diazepam. I was in a cycle of sleeping and waking with this imagery thick in my mind, to the point where alcohol was the only thing that helped drown it out.

In the immediate aftermath, the thought of compensating with alcohol never occurred to me because it was already an integral part of my social life. Unwittingly, I doubled down on my vices and stifled unprocessed grief with nights out, illegal raves and weekend benders. I drank to get drunk, I got high to lift my mood and feel better about myself. Without realising it, I became the first person in the pub on Friday afternoon, and the last person to leave, I become that ubiquitous stranger your pal met in the smoking area of the house party in the wee hours of a Monday morning.

Throughout all of this, I never once considered myself an alcoholic. I'm not sure if I do now. I don't ever *need* a drink, but in my darkest moments, alcohol invariably helped smooth the edges. That's common, of course, but when binge drinking three, four or five times a week, as I was then – that's an issue. I have an addictive personality which, in relation to booze, means that while I can go months on end without a drink, I tend to overindulge when I reintroduce it into my life.

Case in point: the time I spent the night in jail after a heated exchange with a nightclub bouncer. After a few frantic phone calls the following afternoon, I learn that I wasn't solely at fault during the fracas. It transpired I'd been refused entry to the club and was shoved to the floor after protesting – turns out the doorman was quite reactionary in his handling – and I had then quite aggressively sounded off at the doorman, verbally targeting his lack of hair in the process. I'm now bald myself, so I guess the joke's on me.

When Jim died, I wanted nothing more than to get away from everything. I needed some distance between myself and my problems, and therefore Australia, a country nine and a half thousand miles from home, seemed like a good shout.

On May 12, 2009, one year to the day of Jim's passing, I pressed pause on my life by fleeing to Melbourne, where I resided for two years. I returned to Glasgow in mid-2011 in a state of flux regarding work, finances and direction. The feelings I'd shouldered before taking off were effectively put on hold when I left the country and subsequently resurfaced with gusto upon my return. I didn't care that alcohol might be depressing my central nervous system, or the impact that might have on my ever-fluctuating moods. I didn't care that it could reveal or intensify depression, anxiety and shame. If my emotions were numbed along the way, well, I considered that a good thing.

Although primarily associated with physical disease, alcoholism also combines elements of mental illness, and, in the United States it is classified as a substance abuse disorder in the Diagnostic and Statistical Manual of Mental Disorders.[1] In recent years, alcohol was a factor in 3,705 deaths in Scotland, and of the 41,161 patients admitted to hospital that year, 8,509 of those due to mental ill-health were tied to behavioural disorders.[2] Darkly fascinating as those stats are, it wasn't until playing Minority Media's indie video game *Papo & Yo* that I properly understood a tangible link between mental health and alcoholism, and that I could be at risk of being one of those stats. I can't excuse the behaviour that lands people an overnight in jail after too many pints, but *Papo & Yo* made me appreciate the complex relationship that alcohol and mental illness share like nothing before.

Papo & Yo is an autobiographical puzzle-platformer based on the childhood of Vander Caballero, the developer's founder. You play as Quico, an unassuming youth whose unlikely best friend is a huge beast with razor-sharp teeth named Monster. You're tasked with directing your pal through a surrealist South American favela to safety while learning and adjusting to Monster's bouts of hostility when he becomes starved of his supply of poisonous frogs. We later learn that Monster's erratic behaviour reflects that of Caballero's real-life abusive alcoholic father, the poisonous frogs represent alcohol, and the relationship between Quico and Monster is a metaphor for the creator's turbulent childhood.

Having worked in big-budget video games development

for the likes of *FIFA* creator Electronic Arts for several years, Caballero set out on his own to create something that was personal, heartfelt and unique against the growing tide of action shooter adventures that populated the video games landscape at the time. He was clear in his approach to portraying the complexities of addiction in his game.

'I was disappointed with what video games offered players in the way of a wholesome story. Whenever the medium tried to push a story, a narrative, or even a morale it was always done so on a cinematic level. Even the games that set out to craft more interpersonal stories were altered and edited before release in order to maintain that cinematic veneer, whereby changing this or that to suit would ultimately break the game. These limitations still exist today, which is frustrating. I wanted to impress my seven years (at that point) of therapy into a video game, and I wanted to break the mould.'

At face value, *Papo & Yo* is a puzzle-platformer game that has players solving set-pieces, unlocking new areas and avoiding death by Monster.

'In order to make him stop, you have to manipulate your surroundings, you need to stop and think about what's going on, and you're made to consider both your actions and the antagonist's. I used puzzles in order to portray emotional engagement, wherein solving them reflected overcoming emotional quandaries in real life.'

Beneath its simple, fantastical veneer, however, it tells a darker, heavier and credible tale. Caballero believes video games can help people to heal – something he unexpectedly experienced by proxy through countless emails, letters and tweets from fans who related personally to the game's sombre subject matter. It's a two-way street.

So many video games – particularly those within the mainstream spectrum – fail to engage systemic social issues head-on, tending to broach such concerns tangentially if at all. Societal issues, either socio-political or socioeconomic, are usually explored to prop up the functions of genres, and so are rarely scrutinised at any length. We have games like *Max Payne 3*, which depicts its protagonist as an alcoholic, but instead of doing so with empathy, Payne's addiction really only serves to perpetuate a handicap and his image as a stereotypical emotionless lone wolf – glamorising his alcoholism in the way that *The Sopranos* glamorised organised crime. *BioShock*'s portrayal of addiction crudely facilitates its foes in the way of violent, gene tonic-obsessed Splicers; the main character Jack also relies on the drug Eve, the key ingredient of gene tonics, to succeed. Even though it may well be intended as a satirical swipe at Nancy Reagan's "War on Drugs" political campaign of the time, Williams Electronics' '80s classic *NARC* saw the protagonist rid the streets of roaming 'junkies' with a machine gun as a means of combating drug addiction.

Papo & Yo is, thankfully, one example of psychological challenge and exploration done right. Cabalerro explains, 'Therapy is exploration, as is gameplay. I think that video game simulations are the perfect tool where you can actually go back and relive those memories, even if they are painful to you and find a way to cope with them.

'I remember when we were doing focus tests, I had a nine-year old playing *Papo & Yo*. He was playing the prototype and at first the Monster is friendly. It then becomes really aggressive and suddenly I noticed the kid was breathing heavily as he guided the protagonist away from the Monster. He eventually stood upon a rock, out of the Monster's way, and I watched him react to this, using his analytical brain, saying: Why is the Monster like that, how can I help him, how can I survive?

'All of these questions were happening in real-time. The game is there, it's running, it won't stop. Suddenly, whatever he needed to work out in his head, he did. He started interacting with the Monster to calm it down. In a way, this was like real-time therapy. That's the power of video games, and I think that's why people appreciate *Papo & Yo* because it's inspiring the medium of video games to confront a sensitive subject.'

Prior to making *Papo & Yo,* Caballero explained that it was while confiding with a friend – having broken down in tears – that he was told his story was far from unique. What at first seemed lacking in empathy was instead a nudge from his pal that his story could reach people through a video game. That's, of course, what he did, by virtue of – in Caballero's eyes – the most powerful storytelling medium.

More pivotal still is *Papo & Yo's* ending. (▶ ***Spoilers! Skip to the next little flag to avoid.***) Right until the game's final sequence, players are led to believe they can save Monster from his addiction, before ultimately being forced to lead the bumbling co-protagonist to his death. The set-piece is emotive, shocking, and flies in the face of the whimsical heroism intrinsic to most video games.

'That could only happen in a video game, because that whole sequence is driven by its interactivity. You can see similar things in movies or read similar things in books, but in those media, you are passive and it doesn't hit you as hard. When you do so interactively, you really have that hope, you really believe that at some stage you will be able to cure the Monster. And then when it doesn't happen, when you've spent five or so hours getting to that point of realisation that you've spent playing the game, it hits you doubly hard.

'The ending was, in essence, me saying people with addiction can help themselves, but only if they want to. If they don't want to, then the only way the people around them can survive is by letting them go. One of the hardest things you can do in life is letting someone you love go. That's a reality and a statement I wanted to make in the game – that was the only way out. It's pretty hard. I still have people who have suffered from similar situations, from alcoholic or destructive people around them, and they've approached me to tell me how much *Papo & Yo* touched them.'

▶ One of the most interesting stories Caballero recounts involves a father who, while watching his son playing *Papo & Yo* had something of an epiphany. Caballero has no sense if the man was abusive or an alcoholic or not, but the man told him the game made him realise how his son felt whenever he chose to shout at him. In turn, he changed his behaviour and went easier on his son whenever they disagreed – proving that not only can a game like *Papo & Yo* touch victims, it can also reach aggressors.

Like most game developers, Caballero hotly refutes the suggestion that video games make people violent, a rhetoric levied by politicians as far up the chain as the President of the United States of America. Caballero instead believes that gaming's positive and diverse impact will only increase in the years and generations to come as more platforms are developed. Speaking closer to home, creating *Papo & Yo* was liberating, not just for himself but his non-video game-playing family as well.

'If games like *Papo & Yo* or other independent games of a similar ilk were considered in these overblown conversations that are had by politicians in the wake of bad situations, then perhaps public perception – at least, the public who view video games negatively – would be different, and more favourable towards the medium. My family didn't play the game when it launched – they weren't gamers. They did, however, see the videos and they saw the reviews. Overall, they were happy, but it affected them in a very different way to the average player or viewer on YouTube. For them, seeing *Papo & Yo* so well received by the world allowed them to stop feeling ashamed of having a destructive parent. They saw people appreciating the story and sharing their own stories; they realised that they no longer had to be ashamed of suffering at the hands of an alcoholic father. That was a big change for them.'

Vander Caballero's work is an idiosyncratic tale told through the eyes of the creator, but it's done so in a way that allows parallels to be drawn through the lens of loss. Despite my temperamental relationship with alcohol, I have a fantastic relationship with my parents, neither of whom are, or have been, abusive or alcohol-dependent. In turn, *Papo & Yo* marks a milestone in how video games can not only acknowledge addiction but can also serve to educate in an oft-ignored area, whether or not you've experienced it from this point of view. Caballero didn't have the chance to confront his father when he was alive, and instead used his creation as a means of closure.

By its nature, suicide is unexpected, therefore moving on from own loss of Jim was difficult. Against my coping mechanisms following his death; bundling alcohol dependency, a lack of closure and the challenge of letting someone go into one package, allowed me to relate to *Papo & Yo* in ways I didn't expect, which made the experience all the more moving and enlightening.

CHAPTER 5

A QUEST FOR HELP

NARRATIVE & DEPRESSION

While it's not something I'm proud of, my overnight in the cells was a turning point. I don't think I quite realised it at the time, but the event marked the start of my road to relative recovery, as I slowly but surely faced up to myself. I was depressed, clearly, but I don't think I'd realised it before then. I'd experienced suicidal thoughts, but they were just the blues – I wasn't going to act on them, right?

Now, I was beginning to realise things weren't right in my head, but as a twenty-something male living in Glasgow, sharing my feelings wasn't something I'd ever thought possible, far less something I felt able or willing to do. It's a conundrum faced by many Scottish people, especially working class Scottish men,[1] who, to this day, pay strange deference to a warped and outmoded stiff upper lip machismo mentality. At the same time, not long after I'd finished *Papo & Yo*, I discovered two video games that dealt with similarly stark and interpersonal themes, this time directly centred on depression and suicide – Zoe Quinn's *Depression Quest* and Will O'Neill's *Actual Sunlight*. The former is a narrative fiction video game, whereby you play as someone living with depression in everyday life, tasked with managing your illness, your work, your relationships and the daunting prospect of seeking help. I'd eventually seek professional help myself, but it was *Actual Sunlight* that allowed me to process more about Jim's suicide than I ever had on my own. In just four hours of play, I'd ironed out more thoughts in my head than I'd managed in the five years that'd passed since Jim's death. Here was a protagonist who wasn't a hero, wasn't a warrior, wasn't on some profound journey to save the world – but was struggling with similar issues to me, and, in his most sobering moments, struggled with the mundanity of everyday life. I remember the very instant my father – who'd left his interest in video games behind with *Lemmings* on the Atari ST – first fully understood the power of games, when I explained the sombre themes Will O'Neill's work explores, and how I related so closely to them. I took him back to that afternoon when he broke the news of Jim's suicide to me, which was the first time we'd spoken about it since it happened, and I used the video game as a means of outlining the similar thoughts and feelings I'd been coping with. I spent many of my formative years waxing lyrical about video games to my parents, and I was always indulged with polite nods and smiles. But here, for the first time, my dad seemed genuinely interested in the nuts and bolts of this one. There was a glint in his eye and intrigue in his tone, traits otherwise reserved for a cordial chat about his beloved Celtic Football Club, and we connected on a level I hadn't experience before. Father-son bonding is something normally associated with activities and subject matters more pleasant than depression and suicide, but the connection felt nice all the same. In that moment, he better understood one of my passions and how I was feeling, and I was able to share some of my innermost thoughts.

Will O'Neill is an independent video game developer and writer from Toronto, whose work tells mature and dramatic stories that address social and personal issues from realistic perspectives. Through his narrative-heavy games, he carries the mantra that 'people are interested in people', and *changing* those people is what matters to sustain the interest of his players, even if it doesn't necessarily make a difference in what happens to them. O'Neill's debut venture, *Actual Sunlight*, does this via its relatable, everyman protagonist Evan Winter, who's billed as an overweight, lonely and severely depressed young professional. Made with the user-friendly RPG Maker software, O'Neill's work resembles that of a cutesy, whimsical role-playing game, a style closely associated with Japanese-made games such as *Suikoden* and earlier *Final Fantasy* titles. Like *Depression Quest*, his story is delivered almost entirely in text format as it explores the bleak nature of depression, social dysfunction and suicidal tendencies against the daily grind.

'At the time, there weren't many depictions in the media of depression, not only the condition and mental health aspects, but also how it can be affected by circumstances in real life – the working grind and how the realities of everyday life inform depression as well. I felt at the time that every cultural depiction of depression would focus on someone who goes to therapy or turns their life around or goes off on a heroic journey and gets a happy ending.

'I, on the other hand, wanted to depict depression in a way that resonated a lot more personally with me and what I thought was for a lot of people, which is this condition that becomes a part of who you are. You struggle with it, and you might struggle with it for the rest of your life. It can be pretty severe at times, and there's value in being honest about that process – even if honestly about something so sensitive and personal isn't the most reassuring thing.'

Several years on, O'Neill heads his own independent video game development studio and has released a handful of other titles. While his own circumstances are different from when *Actual Sunlight* was introduced to the world, he feels the game's message still resonates today. The landscape of mental health awareness has broadened in scope in the intervening years, he reckons, and mental health issues are more widely discussed in public forums. The public discourse around mental illness is less about genetic defects and dispositions, taboos, or unwieldy thoughts trapped inside our heads, and more about conditions that require professional assessment, levied by the complex interplay of individual circumstance, economic standing and the stresses of day-to-day living.

Before launching *Actual Sunlight*, O'Neill recognised the severity of its content, to the point where he considered it a harrowing piece of art. The thought of triggering players who might have dealt with similar issues themselves didn't occur to him at the time, simply because video games weren't really tackling deep and meaningful issues head-on in this way. *Actual Sunlight* was in turn received with shock and awe by critics – a reception O'Neill mostly expected, once he'd wrapped his head around the acerbity of its message in practice – for its hard-hitting nature and unapologetic tone. Video games that explored themes of depression or poor mental health often did so with a hopeful subtext. They'd tell stories, sure, but they'd reward players for completing gamified criteria with a happy ending dangled like a carrot on a stick as a reward. The protagonist is depressed? Save this character from this compromising situation, fight and defeat this bad guy, and, voila, your soul shall be restored. O'Neill's rebuttal of this was the less than subtle allusion that real life isn't like this, and, quite often, shit happens.

'To be honest, it's easier to create games that project that style of uplifting narrative,' he says. 'In contrast, there's really nothing uplifting about *Actual Sunlight*, but, even at that, I think a lot of people took solace in that fact. They appreciated something that, yes, was gruelling, but, yes, was also honest. In a strange but refreshing way, a lot of players found that encouraging, and I had players tell me they felt better because the game told the truth – even if the truth is horrifying.'

For O'Neill, that very fact was one of the most uplifting things anyone could say about *Actual Sunlight*, which made it a daunting video game for critics to review and comment on. Likewise, recommending the game was difficult. Here's this spritely-looking video game, with friendly-looking characters cutting about in a brightly coloured world, exploring the darkest themes imaginable. It's brutal, yet insightful. Ruthless, yet engaging. Shocking, yet relatable. Beyond depression and suicide, the game also considers the negative ramifications of video game addiction. While the World Health Organisation has formally classified video game addiction as a legitimate mental disorder, in *Actual Sunlight*, this addiction reflects protagonist Evan's spiral into reclusiveness, which in turn underscores the isolating nature of depression. In doing so, O'Neill hoped to pique the interest of gamers and non-gamers alike as he sought to weave relatable real-world themes, such as gambling, around the game's whimsical art style. Doing that led players into a false sense of security. At face value, it looks light-hearted and playful, but beneath its feel-good façade lies its sombre and difficult topics. On a deeper, more profound level, O'Neill believes the fact that *Actual Sunlight looks* like a video game that accentuates its message. Video games are a huge part of avid gamer Evan's life, therefore viewing his life this way is a manifestation of his subconscious and how he might view the world itself. That might sound a bit heavy, but given *Actual Sunlight* is semi-autobiographical, it makes sense. Will O'Neill's breakthrough project could have been developed in many different forms, but for a gamer at heart, there was no more a fitting outlet.

'That's pretty much the converse of the norm – we have so many video games that are based or pull heavily from movies,' O'Neill considers. 'There are so many games that riff shamelessly from TV shows or books and, frankly, it's a pretty theft-happy medium.

'A video game can be chock-full of things that are lifted directly from television and film and no one calls it plagiarism

— they call it inspiration. That's how far out in the ocean video games as a medium are taken. In turn, I thought it was pretty cool do say, no, this should be a video game first and foremost.'

As a narrative-heavy role-playing game, *Actual Sunlight* depicts less action than your average video game. This fits the nature of its goals, setting and themes, as it cracks the lid on what it's like to live with depression, low self-esteem and limited opportunities. Like *Depression Quest*, player choices are limited in *Actual Sunlight* by design, but the feel of living Evan Winter's life, filling his shoes, and directing him around his bleak 9-to-5 existence with a control pad in your hand, to me, feels more impactful than a film or book ever could.

Depression Quest creator Zoe Quinn is a multi-talented American video game developer, programmer, writer and artist, whose breakthrough title reflected her own mental health experiences at the time. *Depression Quest* preceded the Gamergate harassment campaign of 2014, whose supporters subjected a number of women, Quinn included, to months of sustained anonymous and vile abuse, including death and rape threats. By tackling themes outside of the status quo — the violence and shooting found in most mainstream video games — *Depression Quest* was viewed unreasonable by this sect of idiots. This will be the only time Gamergate is mentioned in this book. The mental and psychological effects this hate campaign has impressed on their targets has been profound and devastating, which is why I've chosen to starve the perpetrators of attention beyond this paragraph, provided for context only.

In Quinn's own words, *Depression Quest* 'aims to show other sufferers of depression that they are not alone in their feelings, and to illustrate to people who may not understand the illness the depths of what it can do to people.'

While *Depression Quest's* themes and subject matter are dark, its interface is streamlined and its central mechanic simple – when placed in relatable real world situations, you're given a selection of numbered options regarding how you wish to respond. Through your choices, the game throws up over 150 unique encounters, all dependent on the decisions you make. As your mental state fluctuates, specific, seemingly innocuous paths become closed in order to reflect the plight of people with depression.

Here's a direct except from an early *Depression Quest* scenario, where a friend has casually asked if you, the protagonist, is feeling okay:

Do you...

1. Suggest a change of location and confide in her honestly

2. Test the waters and open up a little, hoping she'll understand

3. Insist that nothing is wrong and change the subject

4. Defensively ask what she means by that

5. Notice that your hands are shaking

- You are deeply depressed. Even activities you used to enjoy hold little or no interest for you, and you exist in a near constant state of lethargy.

- You are currently not seeing a therapist.

- You are currently not taking medication for depression.

Despite being feasible and arguably *better* answers to the friend's question, *Depression Quest* intentionally prevents the player from selecting the first two, illustrating the obstructive effect depression can have. In direct reference to my own situation – and having also spoken to a number of video game players that also suffer from depressive tendencies since – Quinn's ground-breaking work balances voyeurism and relatability with aplomb and really captures the essence of depression in a whole manner of mundane, day-to-day circumstances.

★ ★ ★

On April 24, 2012, I visited my doctor and told him I was depressed. I told him I was certain it was a result of my uncle's suicide, and that I wanted to seek professional help. I'm sure there are more exciting ways to spend your 26th birthday, but this was a big step towards feeling better. I'd love to tell you there was one profound and epiphanic moment that led me to this decision, but there wasn't. By this point, hardly an hour went by without me thinking of Jim. I thought about the uncle I loved and missed, and I thought about the brutal nature of his passing. I obsessed over how he'd have looked after slipping away, and how horrifying that must have been for the neighbour that found him. I thought about his humanist funeral, the modest group of people that gathered in the parlour, and how heavy his coffin was when I helped carry him to his grave. In the present, everything reminded me of his death too. I became ultra-sensitive to even the vaguest allusions to suicide in television shows and films, and learned to loathe the throwaway quip 'I wanted to kill myself', which, suddenly, everyone I knew appeared to use more often than before. Swallowed by this self-built whirlwind of irrationality, I was exhausted. I was crabbit. I was constantly anxious and I was a nightmare to live with. I can't apologise to my girlfriend, and long-suffering roommate Jenny enough.

Through all of this, making first contact with the doctor made sense. There wasn't one singular moment that drove the decision, but loads of small and tiring ones. My doctor was great, which I realise makes me very lucky. For him to be so understanding, sympathetic and empathetic from the outset put many of my anxieties tied specifically to seeking help, at ease. He gave me information pamphlets about counselling and anti-depressant medication to pore over at home, pointed me towards various mental health websites, recommended online forums I might find useful. He suggested a handful of psychologists who specialised in everything from cognitive behavioural therapy to emotion-focused therapy, interpersonal therapy and psycho-dynamic therapy. I left my doctor's office that afternoon buoyed by my achievement. Then I didn't seek the help that was on offer for another two years.

Seeking help for issues of mental health is a very difficult thing, but following through is even harder. That's something hardly anyone talks about. Getting through the doctor's door isn't easy, but sticking around, pursuing that next step, visiting a therapist, committing to mood-altering drugs for the foreseeable future is a different thing entirely.

As a society, we've made some great strides since the turn of the millennium in encouraging mental health discussion, but I still feel we're too quick to offer soundbites that say *I'm always here to talk. Reach out. Seek help.* These are great, but I never hear anyone saying, *I'm still here, keep reaching out and keep working with the help.* In the marathon of mental health, sprinting from the starting line with cheers of support is wonderful, but it's those handing out bottles of water and high-fives on mile twenty that really keep you going. To this end, I had, perhaps naively, assumed telling my doctor how I was feeling would mean that everything else would naturally follow. Once I had everything laid out in front of me, the thought of putting my mental health right suddenly felt very real and very intimidating. I wanted to talk about the shit in my head, but I'd grown familiar with my own depression. I channelled my omnipresent anxiety into hitting university coursework deadlines and working my arse off in my spare time building the foundations of a freelance writing career. I was irritable around other people but I found the fog of depression weirdly helpful in focusing on specific tasks, probably as a means of distraction. The next step was into the unknown, however, and that was terrifying. *Depression Quest* and *Actual Sunlight* helped me organise the thoughts in my head, and gave that confidence to follow through on everything my doctor had relayed. It took me until May 2014 before I first started a rolling prescription of Citalopram anti-depressant and anti-anxiety medication, and sessions with a psychiatrist. I still take medication today, and while I didn't find therapy as helpful as other people I've since spoken to, I formed an understanding of the process and an appreciation of talking through your problems with a qualified stranger.

In the intervening period, I discovered the work of Eli Piilonen – a Nebraska-based indie developer responsible for two puzzle-platformers named *The Company of Myself* and its prequel *Fixation*. Both feature protagonists who want to seek professional help but are faced with metaphorical obstacles, depicted in-game by actual puzzles and conundrums the player must overcome as they move closer to receiving the treatment they need. Hurdling these puzzles lets you unlock part of the protagonists' narratives and take a step closer to each one's eventual resolution. In essence, Piilonen's game portrays the challenges of speaking out about mental health and, as I learned first-hand, the challenges of ascertaining treatment.

'It happened sort of organically,' Piilonen shares on his focus on the process of seeking help for mental health issues. 'There was a certain type of content in movies and in stories that I really liked that I didn't see happening in the games I was playing.'

Prior to designing *The Company of Myself*, Piilonen wanted to make a game that incorporated puzzle elements and real-world character studies. In doing so, he crafted an interesting character-cloning mechanic, whereby players are encouraged to fail several times on specific levels, before restarting and using their previous incarnations – represented by shadows – to reach otherwise inaccessible areas. Some levels limit your retries, whereas others offer unlimited restarts.

'I wanted to discover a mechanic where you're collaborating with yourself. The lead character is someone suffering from social anxiety and tends to keep himself to himself. I felt at the time I'd come upon this naturally, but then in retrospect, I was just sitting around making flash games, doing a bunch of little things I didn't totally know how to do.

'Maybe this is confirmation bias, but I feel like if you accidentally put yourself in the story, that's the best way. If you're actively trying to tell a story about yourself, it might feel really awkward and stilted. But if you write about stuff that you feel is interesting and you write about stuff that's important to you and you realise later that it's actually extremely embarrassing, that you were divulging all of this stuff. I think that works best.'

The Company of Myself suggests failure is okay, that being unsure or introverted is normal, but sometimes coming out of yourself and facing uncertain circumstances is necessary to ensure your wellbeing. *Fixation* expands on its forerunner's conceit with the inclusion of more sophisticated dialogue and puzzles, and more rounded non-playable characters.

'Making a game is a way for me to discuss stuff that I can't talk about in casual conversation usually,' continues Piilonen. 'If it's something that's too uncomfortable, I find it's easier for me to put that into a game instead of gambling on whether or not someone is going to be like, *oh this isn't dinner conversation.*'

It's here that both *Fixation* and *The Company of Myself* excel. They're simple in aesthetics and design, but their core sentiment is one which is not only informative but, crucially, relatable. The idea that both games mimic character studies adds a dose of realism to the message they send as they simultaneously engage players with intuitive platforming so as to avoid over-egging their premise. At no point does either of the games lecture the player, their messages are more; here's a thing which isn't ideal, here's what you can do and here's how you might go about it.

'I think it really is that feeling of solidarity. That no matter what your life is like, you can feel really good about it, you can feel really bad about it. When you feel really bad about it, it's really easy to forget that a whole bunch of people have had very similar experiences and who'd agree about how much whatever thing is hurtful or how much it sucks or how much it's affecting you. The solidarity that someone else agrees that this particular thing is uncomfortable, I think, in turn, is very comforting.'

Piilonen acknowledges video games as a medium are constantly evolving and that while he's well aware not everyone is interested in games that explore deeper, more cultured themes, the feedback he's received over the years makes it worthwhile – if for nothing else but to prove he and other players are not alone.

'There are rare cases where someone sends us a thing that's super heartfelt and gives a really clear, tangible example of a way that we really helped. It's this super unexpected benefit from typing on a computer and learning how to solve these technical problems that makes it worth it.'

Shortly after playing *The Company of Myself*, I finally booked in with a counsellor, and got myself on long-term SSRI (selective serotonin reuptake inhibitor) medication. I then contacted Piilonen to let him know that his work encouraged me to finally seek professional help.

★ ★ ★

After creating such a personal, touching and sobering video game in *Actual Sunlight*, it would have been easy for Will O'Neill to change tact. Working on something lighter in tone and nature would surely have been justified. Instead, he created *Little Red Lie* – another narrative adventure that takes the core themes of his previous work and extends them to the plight of friends and family.

One damning characteristic of my own depression is selfishness, which made *Little Red Lie*'s exploration of how this can affect those around you instantly relatable. It also proved O'Neill to not be a one-hit wonder, but to be someone committed to his message, able to hone in on the granular details of depression from more than one perspective. Being consumed by overwhelming thoughts is one of the most debilitating aspects of depression and anxiety. It's hard not to become obsessed with how you're feeling because of how desperate and defeated both conditions can make you feel – none of which is good for your spouse, partner, family or friends. I have a great support network who've helped me through my struggles, but living with someone shrouded by a dark cloud can't be easy. Being side-by-side with someone whose moods can swing out of control in a moment's notice, who snaps, who goes inside themselves, who can be overly sensitive but not sensitive enough towards others. Depression is a waking nightmare but living with someone with depression comes with its own checklist of challenges.

During my darkest spells, I learned that Jenny has an uncanny knack for walking on eggshells. At my worst, I snapped at anything and everything. No milk in the fridge, no petrol in the car, no gas in the meter – all of which were as much my responsibility as they were Jenny's. My mood was up, then down, then up and down again. I was a living, fuming, volcanic yo-yo. I was unpredictable, temperamental, and a general pain in the arse to live with. Jenny did everything in her power to avoid upsetting me and was still on the receiving end of my bullshit too often that I could ever realise. Besides all of this being wholly unfair, looking back, Jenny's ability to defuse situations and bring me back from the brink is all the more impressive given she was more often than not, at the end of her own exhausting week of tight university deadlines and long, gruelling hours as a restaurant waitress. Once again, to Jenny, I'm sorry.

O'Neill's *Little Red Lie* tackles this dynamic of living with depression head-on by folding debt and deception into its narrative-focused, interactive fiction experience. Players are encouraged to lie to themselves and to others, as they follow the stories of two protagonists – one, a poor and family-re-liant millennial named Sarah Stone, and another, a deceitful businessman named Arthur Fox.

'The real germ of the idea was that I wanted to write a game about family, and I wanted to make a game about how mental health impacts not just the person, but how it echoes outwards to the people around the individual who is suffering. In *Little Red Lie*, the character of Melissa, the protagonist Sarah's sister, is very much intended to be like Evan Winter from *Actual Sunlight*, but seen from the outside, from how Sarah sees her, and how someone from the outside might see them and observe and cope and deal with the effect of living with someone like that can ripple out.

'A lot of the crisis within the Stone family stems from Melissa, even though the game is centred around Sarah. That was a big part of what made me want to do it. From there, I started to think about honesty within families and economic circumstances overall. The end product was a game about depression and debt in an age where both concepts are omnipresent. I wanted to explore how economic circumstances can impact mental health, and also how they might impact the future – one filled with further economic precarity.

'That huge transition is still to take place between the Baby Boom generation and their relative prosperity – in Western cultures, at least – and their children, who were brought up to believe that we'd have a bright future if we played by the rules, went to college, paid into a pension scheme, and so on and so forth, and how that's ultimately all going to fall apart.'

Little Red Lie starts out with a greater focus on Sarah, but slowly begins to introduce the shady and affluent lifestyle of Arthur. O'Neill posits that while most players will instantly identify with the former, the latter exists to contextualise the debt most working-class people shoulder, and the disparity in wealth and morals between those folk and the higher echelons of society. With its onus on family, how people with depression force their afflictions on those closest to them, and the same tied to lifelong debt *Little Red Lie* is both hideously relatable and so dark that O'Neill observed a distinct chasm between those willing to openly identify with *Actual Sunlight*'s themes and this follow up.

'If I look at the reviews of *Little Red Lie* – from critics and players – I think the majority of people got a sense of what I was going for,' O'Neill adds. 'But throughout, there's definitely an absence of people saying *Yes, I played this and I identify with it*. That's interesting because I think it shows the difference between the two games. In *Actual Sunlight* you saw a lot of people standing up and admitting that they too suffer from depression, anxiety and perhaps even suicidal thoughts or tendencies.

'Generally speaking, people would get a sympathetic or supportive response to that. That's far less stigmatic than saying *Yeah, you know what, I probably am going to be financially-dependant on my family for the rest of my life and there's nothing I can do about it*. That is way darker and shameful in our culture; the interesting thing is that's becoming more and more common in modern society. It's you and everyone you know, especially for people in this generation.'

I related so closely to *Little Red Lie* on a personal level that it made me cringe. I thought of everything I had and was putting Jenny through. So blinded was I by own my own afflictions that I couldn't see it – but here was *Little Red Lie* putting me in the shoes of character that held a mirror up to my own behaviour. The creeping realisation that, aye, depression is shite, but *it's not just shite for you* washed over, thicker than the dark fog that perpetually followed me around at that point in my life. I saw through new eyes the strength and patience of Jenny for the crap she had put up with through the process.

In Scotland, it's estimated that only 57 per cent of people would be willing to have a relationship with another person who has a mental health problem,[2] and while part of facing up to depression, anxiety or whichever mental illness you suffer from is about owning your afflictions, those closest will invariably shoulder some of that along the way. The UK's Mental Health Foundation suggests the best way for people to support partners with depression is simply to be patient and understanding. It advises that they listen, read-up and educate themselves, and encourage professional help. It also stresses partners should try not to take any negativity levied at them to heart. Fortunately for me, Jenny did all of these things, but not for a second did any of it come easy. Despite being a bit of a dick in the depths of my depression, I've always been open with Jenny about my feelings and thoughts, which I'm certain helped us over the course. If you've found yourself in a similar situation, Couple Therapy for Depression – a type of talking therapy that can help people with both relationship and mental health difficulties between partners – is a more formalised option you might consider. Against cognitive behavioural therapy's (CBT) 44 per cent recovery rate for couples seeking profession help together, Couple Therapy for Depression sits at 52 per cent. Consider this food for thought, which is surely better than ranting about empty milk cartons. Things can change – for Will O'Neill, it was creating his games that allowed him to contextualise his own mental health, and deal with the boundaries and limitations of these changes, and what actually remains ever-present.

'Mental health has been a shifting topic as I've gotten older. I'm in my mid-30s now, and there are some things that you accept about yourself and you realise that by this stage, they're probably not going to change.

'You need to reconcile yourself with that, in your personal life, in your professional life, adulthood is in many ways solving one problem after another. I find that long-term problems and deeper existential questions of mental health turn into background noise. That's not to say I ignore them, but I accept them as omnipresent in everything that I do.'

The realisation that mental health issues could be permanent was a big moment for me. It's always comforting to know that through therapy – be that talking to a professional or reaching out to a friend of family member – and monitored medication, I'm in a position to stay on top of my depression and anxiety, but it's equally daunting to think how things may go if I remove them from my life entirely.

Through all of this, I've come to learn just how stigmatised mental health issues are, even today, and how counter-productive this can be to the wider discussion.

Personally, Jim's death has made me extra sensitive to the ways in which suicide is portrayed in modern media, and I often compare how television, films and books make me feel when handling the subject to how it felt first-hand. There's a particularly harrowing scene towards the end of *The Sopranos*, for example. (▶ *Spoilers! Skip to the next little flag to avoid.*) One of the show's key characters wants to quit the mob but is denied the request by his boss, the series' protagonist, Tony Soprano. Dejected, the character then hangs himself in his garage. The scene drags out for dramatic effect and I found it all very difficult to watch, as it portrayed the act with the bleakness and raw despondence of the real thing.

▶ Video games, especially the work of Piilonen and O'Neill, helped me seek help towards my mental health, but it wasn't easy. When I first flirted with the idea of seeing a doctor, I knew nothing. I didn't know where to start, and when I did start, I got off on the wrong foot. Before first consulting my GP, I discovered an NHS-run mental health initiative in Glasgow named Steps, and, almost immediately, fell out with a receptionist. When I arrived at the centre within which Steps operated, I asked the woman at the desk if I was in the correct building. She didn't answer me, not directly, and instead sang *Tragedy* at me, her hands raised, miming the well-known chore-ographed dance and all. I can laugh about it now, but I felt stupid and insignificant in the moment. Stumbling blocks like this are exactly why people in this part of the world don't talk about mental illness.

Another part of the problem is the fact mental illness is often invisible. If you were to break your leg, stave your finger, or roll your ankle, you'd likely book an appointment with your GP, or visit Accident and Emergency or Minor Injuries at the hospital. You learn this as early as primary school age – that if you're stricken with a physical injury or sickness, there's a school nurse waiting to patch you up and make you right. Maybe schools are better at it now, but I was never once taught about mental health at secondary school. I did learn how to apply a condom on a banana, though, for whatever that is worth.

And so it took video games, the escape I was interested in most, to give me the gentle nudge I needed towards addressing my faltering mental health. Five years after I left school, Jim died. Six years after that, I'd started therapy and my first round of anti-depressant medication. Six years again after that and here I am writing a book about mental health and video games that, who knows, your children might have access to in their school library. No matter your age, no matter the age of anyone in your life, video games can be a catalyst towards that one crucial step towards seeking help.

A NEW CHALLENGER APPEARS

LAUREN AITKEN

Lauren is a Scottish journalist who works as a Guides Writer for video games website VG24/7. Her first foray into playing video games came during the '90s via Sonic the Hedgehog *and the SEGA Mega Drive, before graduating to the likes of* The Elder Scrolls IV: Oblivion, The Elder Scrolls V: Skyrim, *the* Mass Effect *trilogy and* The Witcher 3 *on PC a couple of decades down the line.*

Between Mass Effect *and* The Witcher 3, *Lauren has used video games to cope with being diagnosed with Emotionally Unstable Personality Disorder, and with the loss of a child during a second trimester miscarriage.*

'The first console we got as a family was a SEGA Mega Drive, with *Sonic The Hedgehog.* We then got a PlayStation and, as two wee girls, my dad stopped us from playing shooter games and anything overly violent. We played platformers like *Toy Story 2, Crash Bandicoot,* and *Spyro The Dragon.*

'That was my introduction to gaming, and it wasn't until I was in my early 20s that I was introduced into PC gaming and got into *The Elder Scrolls IV: Oblivion*. That game took up a lot of my time, but looking back, I really wasn't well at that time in my life. I was undiagnosed, I was running about a bit of a riot. I have to say, 2011-2014 is a bit of a blur for me. Between *Oblivion* and *Mass Effect*, I became absorbed in those games and lost track of my life. In many ways, I saw the character in *Mass Effect* as my friend, daft as that sounds, because I became so emotionally invested with everything. I was unemployed, I was depressed, I wasn't looking after myself, and I had to pull away from it a little bit.

'I went cold turkey at that point. I had to ask myself, as an adult woman, how could I lose part of my life to video games? I now play on PC and PlayStation 4 every day. I use for them for work, and I think I've got a much healthier relationship with games now. I'm now in a position where I can set a limit and stop.

'Still, when you write about games for a living, the line between what's done for pleasure and what's done for work can become very blurred. Writing about games from home for a living sounds fun, until you realise you're doing so alone and you don't see anyone for weeks at a time.

'Several years later, with the virtue of hindsight and despite the fact I was playing the games too much at the time, I still view my time engrossed in the *Mass Effect* games as a positive experience. Before then, I'd enjoyed *Oblivion*, I'd enjoyed *Skyrim*, but up until that point, I'd never played a role-playing game where the voiced character made their own relationships.

'In terms of my own mental health experiences, I'll keep it quite brief. I experienced trauma when I was younger, which was a huge proponent of it. I was a sensitive child, I turned into a bit of a strange adult, I struggled with having a sense of self, relationships, trusting people. Nothing was done about any of this in my teens I was told that I'd grow out of it. Of course, you don't just grow out of these things, and they continue to manifest until the point where I became really unwell. I was hospitalised, and then people were saying, *hey, maybe there is actually something wrong here. Maybe she's not at it.* You know what Scottish people are like, the first thought is never that it might be mental health related but instead that you don't want to work or that you're just a bit lazy.

'My first diagnosis (Emotionally Unstable Personality Disorder, otherwise known as Borderline Personality Disorder) was made in 2017, after I'd been unwell in 2016, at which stage I'd basically reached breaking point. From there, I got treatment. Like anything, you get better, you recover. I'm in a much better place now.

'*The Witcher 3* came out in 2015, and in 2014, I had a second trimester miscarriage. That blew me out of the water. It was an unplanned pregnancy, so to have an unplanned loss was a bit of a double whammy. Away from real life, I'd seen *The Witcher 3* promotional trailer and I really fancied it. I started playing it shortly after my bad news, knew very little about the game, besides the fact it looked banging and before long reached the Bloody Baron's Family Matters quest.

(▶ *Spoilers! Skip to the next little flag on page 117 to avoid.*)

The end of this particular quest culminates in a pretty gruesome unexpected pregnancy and loss.

'I remember at the time, playing this quest and being really angry. I remember thinking: how dare a game do this? Having played *Mass Effect*, *Skyrim*, *Oblivion*, all these games that were built around choice and upset and real life scenarios, this felt so cold. And I actually mean cold in a positive way, because I'd never seen a game take on a subject so personal to so many people, real life abortions, real life pregnancy loss, real life abuse. The Baron character, you could see through him. You knew he was going to be an abuser, but how he reacted to the baby, how Anna, the mother, reacted to the baby; how the player was given the option of dealing with the baby – that you could either let it become a monster, or put it out of its pain and free its spirit… It was all framed by fantasy, but the whole segment moved me and helped me deal with my own real world anger.

'I'd pushed all of that out of the way, but being able to see this play out in video game, I don't know, it offered me a sense of closure that I don't think I could have got from any other medium. Nobody helped me deal with the grief of an unplanned pregnancy and loss, possibly because there was no grief for anybody else. Not really. There was grief for me being in pain, but no real grief for the baby. *The Witcher 3* gave me, as a player, the choice to fight or free the spirit of the baby – which meant it was named and buried. Anyone who's dealt with premature loss will be familiar with this, but the hospital gives you the option to keep the remains if you want, but also to take them away and dispose of them themselves.

► 'At 23 years old, being asked, *Do you want to keep the remains of your dead baby?* That's a difficult question to be asked. I was more, *Na, you deal with that, thanks*. I didn't name my baby, I didn't deal with any of the after effects, so playing this mission made me return to my doctor and be like, *Actually, can somebody tell me why this happened?* I had so many questions that'd been left answered. I found out the baby was a boy, the loss had been a result of a chromosome defect related to the heart, and I was told it was super unlikely to happen again.

'Skip to the modern day, and Greg and I are going through fertility treatment. We've not managed to conceive. The tests keep coming back saying it's not related to what I went through before, it's just bad luck. Still, I'm in the position now where I'm more open-minded about the whole thing. I look back at my experience and believe *The Witcher 3* helped me accept that while the baby has gone, it turned into a wee spirit and went back into the ether, the sphere, whatever you want to call it. At the time, when I first played that mission, I admittedly had to stop playing the game for about three weeks. I was just so bloody angry at it! How dare a game elicit that emotion? How dare a game touch on something so profound and so taboo? I didn't ever expect a game to touch on these themes, and to touch on them so well and thorough. It wasn't just a throwaway comment buried somewhere, it was: *we're going to make you fucking do this*.

'I can't think of any TV show where I've seen loss portrayed so violently and in your face. That's the beauty of modern games. They give you more choices that are more realistic. I think that's the thing that affects more people now. These quandaries extend beyond the fantastical stuff, and go far closer to the bone. They challenge the granular, itty-bitty decisions of life. For me, I find that helpful.'

CHAPTER 6

WHO AND YOU

GAMING RELATIONSHIPS & GAMING DISORDER

We can all agree that anxiety is a mental illness. And depression. And OCD. And many others. But, when it comes to video games and mental health, there is a more contentious topic that it would be remiss not to discuss: gaming disorder.

We've seen video games being rubbished by the media as dangerous and a bad influence, but when the World Health Organisation (WHO) calls for caution from a medical standpoint, people listen. In its 11th Revision of the International Classification of Disease – approved in May 2019, set to become official as of January 2022 – the WHO officially labelled video games as potentially harmful to its players.

Many in the gaming industry, including myself, have their concerns. Here, I want to explore the three topics that struck me as pertinent upon hearing of this new classification:

1. The potential overlap between in-game gambling-style 'loot boxes' (a consumable virtual item which can be redeemed through specific gameplay to receive a randomised selection of further virtual items) and 'real-life' gambling,

2. The absence of clarification as to whether the casual gamer who may game for relaxation and escapism is viewed by the WHO in the same nature as a diagnosed addict, and,

3. The risk that future generations of budding gaming enthusiasts might disengage and miss out due to the stigma that can rise from gaming being seeing as an officially classified danger.

Before diving deeper, here's an introduction from the Q&A on WHO's website on Gaming Disorder, in their own words, to understand exactly what we're dealing with:

What is gaming disorder?

Gaming disorder is defined as a pattern of gaming behavior ("digital-gaming" or "video-gaming") characterized by impaired control over gaming, increasing priority given to gaming over other activities to the extent that gaming takes precedence over other interests and daily activities, and continuation or escalation of gaming despite the occurrence of negative consequences.

For gaming disorder to be diagnosed, the behaviour pattern must be of sufficient severity to result in significant impairment in personal, family, social, educational, occupational or other important areas of functioning and would normally have been evident for at least 12 months.

Should all people who engage in gaming be concerned about developing gaming disorder?

Studies suggest that gaming disorder affects only a small proportion of people who engage in digital- or video-gaming activities. However, people who partake in gaming should be alert to the amount of time they spend on gaming activities, particularly when it is to the exclusion of other daily activities, as well as to any changes in their physical or psychological health and social functioning that could be attributed to their pattern of gaming behaviour.

In response to this new classification, a host of gaming organisations came together to refute the idea that video games as a form are inherently more addictive than other media. This was co-signed by The Association for UK Interactive Entertainment (UKIE), the European Games Developer Association (EGDF), the Entertainment Software Association (ESA), the Korea Association of Game Industry (K-GAMES), the Entertainment Software Association of Canada (ESAC), the Interactive Games and Entertainment Association (IGEA), the Interactive Software Federation of Europe (ISFE), and Brazil's União Brasileira de Vídeo e Games (UBV&G).

Video games across all kinds of genres, devices and platforms are enjoyed safely and sensibly by more than 2 billion people worldwide, with the educational, therapeutic, and recreational value of games being well-founded and widely recognised. We are therefore concerned to see 'gaming disorder' still contained

*in the latest version of the WHO's ICD-11 despite signif-
icant opposition from the medical and scientific community.
The evidence for its inclusion remains highly contested and
inconclusive.*

*We hope that the WHO will reconsider the mounting
evidence put before them before proposing inclusion of 'gaming
disorder' in the final version of ICD-11 to be endorsed next
year. We understand that our industry and supporters around
the world will continue raising their voices in opposition to this
move and urge the WHO to avoid taking steps that would
have unjustified implications for national health systems across
the world.*

With the groundwork set out, onto my first concern:
What could this classification mean for those with diagnosed
addictive personalities, through the lens of an overlap between
loot boxes and 'real-life' gambling?

I have an extended family member who struggles with a
drug addiction, I've said earlier that I've relied on alcohol in
times of crisis, and I hold the view that drugs should be decrim-
inalised and treated as a national health issue in the hope that
no one ever has to become an addict. When I was studying
at university, I worked in a Glasgow pub where some patrons,
lovely as they were, would start drinking at 8am and still be sat
there guzzling Guinness, White and Mackay and Tennent's Lager
at 8pm. They'd complain about the heroin addicts who often
hung around the local area trying to flog whatever knocked-off
high street wares they could to fund their next fix.

One particularly aggrieved customer leaned over the bar where I was mopping up, him being seven hours deep into a Tuesday afternoon session. 'Know what I'd do? Round the junkies up on an island and burn the lot of them. They're a waste of fucking space.'

This is, obviously, a particularly obtuse and offensive view of drug addiction, but, in my own experience, it isn't uncommon. My response to this and similar lines of thought is that no one willingly chooses that life. No one wakes up and says *You know what? Stealing tellies, selling pirate DVDs up Glasgow's Gallowgate and sleeping rough looks like a great old time.* It's a complicated ecosystem harbouring cycles of destruction not helped by country-wide austerity – there's not enough room in this book to do this topic justice (nor do I pretend to have the expertise). I just know that I believe addicts are victims of circumstance, and their vices consume them, not the other way around.

So, can virtual elements within video games actually be addictive, as much as these tangible substances and experiences? Video game developers *are* getting increasingly better at creating games that encourage players to return time and time again. One of the most recognised and longest serving examples of subscription-based gaming is *World of Warcraft*, a massive multi-player online role-playing game (MMORPG), that was released in 2004 by Blizzard Entertainment. The fantasy MMORPG is still going strong today, having grossed $9.23 billion (£7 billion) as of 2017,[1] and having added dozens of paid-for expansion packs that have grown its world beyond recognition since inception. It's a common theme among games.

In his article, 'It's time to stop running from gaming addiction', Eurogamer's Deputy Editor Wesley Yin-Poole, argues that the WHO's moves to classify gaming addiction via Gaming Disorder was entirely reasonable, and that pushback from video game trade organisations was embarrassing.[2] Yin-Poole did so within a heartfelt, candid and very personal essay on his own perceived *World of Warcraft* addiction in 2005, how he struggled to maintain employment in the throes of the all-consuming game, and risked losing his relationship to his now wife and mother of his children.

'Video games are brilliant and fun and have educational, therapeutic and recreational value, just as this joint statement points out,' writes Yin-Poole, 'but they are also complex, often problematic, sometimes cynical and occasionally exploitative.'

Yin-Poole suggests that by medically recognising video games as potentially addictive, it could in turn put game developers under pressure to avoid certain mechanics and design elements that can encourage reckless patterns at the player's end. The introduction and popularity of loot boxes is one such mechanic which muddies the waters of a blanket argument that games aren't addictive by introducing monetised gambling elements into, often otherwise, innoucous titles. These consumable virtual items are gained via a kind of in-game gambling and a luck that can be traded for randomised in-game wares, aesthetic items, and passes which grant access to desireable functions. Loot boxes, and variations on the theme, have appeared in a number of popular games in recent years, including Blizzard's *Overwatch,* EA Sports' *FIFA* football series; Valve's *Team Fortress 2,* Psyonix's *Rocket League,* and Electronic Arts' *Star Wars Battlefront*

II. Monetisation in Epic Games' 2017 runaway megahit *Fortnite: Battle Royale* comes in the form of its Battle Pass feature. While the game itself is free to play, its Battle Passes are obtained via its in-game currency, V-Bucks, and can either be purchased with real-world money, or earned in *Battle Royale's* sister game *Fortnite: Save the World*, which costs $40/£32.99 for its no-frills "Standard Founders Pack". The opportunity to unlock 100 tiers of in-game extras with this Battle Pass, which enhances their playing experience is naturally appealing.

Gambling laws vary from country to country, but while the likes of the Netherlands and Belgium have come down hard on loot boxes – players in these regions can no longer purchase loot boxes in Valve's *Counter-Strike: Global Offensive* by law, for example – the UK has adopted a less forthright approach. In September 2019, the Department for Digital, Culture Media and Sport recommended that the UK government regulate loot boxes under the Gambling Act 2005, but the Gambling Commission deemed loot boxes not to be gambling because players cannot 'cash out' items – despite there being a number of readily available third-party sites and services that do so online. Still, many companies including Microsoft, Sony, Nintendo, and latterly, *Fortnite's* Epic Games committed to a transparency in loot boxes initiative that requires video game developers to publicly disclose the 'rarity or probability' of obtaining certain items at random, so people can see the odds they're actually faced with.

The discussion surrounding loot boxes has extended to the medical field, where NHS England's National Mental Health Director Claire Murdoch called for tighter scrutiny over them and virtual monetisation – particularly in games aimed at or played by young children. 'Frankly, no company should be setting kids up for addiction by teaching them to gamble on the content of these loot boxes,' she says in an article published on the NHS website. 'No firm should sell to children loot box games with this element of chance, so yes, those sales should end. Young people's health is at stake, and although the NHS is stepping up with these new, innovative services, we cannot do this alone, so other parts of society must do what they can to limit risks and safeguard children's wellbeing.'[3]

While the NHS cannot tackle this issue alone, it also can't be considered in a purely black and white approach. For Yin-Poole, the route forward is in analysing video game addiction, as opposed to denying it outright. His article continues, 'Underneath it all, I think the reaction to the WHO's gaming disorder is about the fear of facing up to uncomfortable truths about game design. We celebrate games that are addictive but we refuse to call them addictive, even though they have been designed to be exactly that. Developers want you to become addicted to their games, which is understandable because if people are hooked on your game it suggests it's really fucking good.

'The grind, loot, loot boxes, levelling up, infinite progression, prestige, battle passes, experience points, the numbers, the numbers and even more numbers, all going up – this is the guts of popular video games today. Keep us in the game, keep us engaged, keep us caring and then the recurring revenue rolls in. In this context, it seems reasonable that something along the lines of a gaming disorder might actually be a useful thing to think about.'

No matter which side you fall on the classification debate, this is a valid point. Studies have suggested that loot boxes are linked to 'problem gambling',[4] [5] which does indicate a trend – but often a case-by-case basis, like any other form of gambling or potentially addictive activity. Saying this, it's an area which shouldn't be trivialised. As a parent, I particularly worry that free access to loot boxes and the lottery obtaining their contents sends the wrong message to kids, and also that they will be naturally inclined to want something their friends have that they don't. When I was at school, two stripe Adidas tracksuit bottoms or fake Nike sneaks would have justified a playground crucifixion, and I could imagine similar rules applying to the latest premium *Fortnite* skin from a loot box today. It's with this in mind that I'm pleased to hear a host of major publishers and platform holders – not least Microsoft, Sony and Nintendo – have agreed to start publishing loot box odds in all of their games by the end of 2020. It's all a step in the right direction.

The question remains: is there a conflation between the addictive characteristics of games with the battles of real-life addiction, or is there indeed a correlation? Do these virtual worlds and the potential gambling elements of loot boxes qualify as addiction severely enough to fit into the WHO's classification? It's hard to say, simply because addiction treats every person differently. At the time of publication, some governments and organisations believe that loot boxes qualify as gambling and should be treated as such. In the UK, the Gambling Commission does not.[6] Even at the highest level, there's no definitive consensus that can easily be agreed on; it's a topic we need continued research and analysis in, as Yin-Poole suggests, not a blanket 'for' or 'against' approach.

★ ★ ★

Another of my concerns is that we're mistaking video game escapism for avoidance, investment for addiction. There's no clear distinction given as to whether the casual gamer, who turns to games for escapism and to relax, would be viewed similarly to a diagnosed addict. As someone who does regularly turn to video games as a coping tool, should I be classified an addict?

My concern of WHO's stance comes from a very personal, possibly selfish perspective – I was raised on video games and owe so much of my personal development to them. In the wake of Jim's suicide, they provided me with an outlet that I couldn't find in any other part of my life at that time. They offered me refuge and a degree of escapism in ways that football, socialising or conversation with friends and family just couldn't. Games were my survival, and continue to be my way to take a step back when overwhelmed. Am I an addict? Am I alone in this?

'Growing up, I often used video games as an escape,' Dr Umran Ali, senior lecturer in Creative Media at the University of Salford, tells me. 'I came from a quite a tough, working-class background and games were both educational for me and a pathway to a different life to my own at the time. Video games are transformative, so, from a personal perspective, I'm quite angry that the World Health Organisation have classified "gaming addiction", as a mental health disorder, mainly because of how dangerous that label is, and the way it ties into how games have always been perceived by some people.

'I was thinking about other hobbyist interests and I thought of football,' Ali muses. 'I thought about football hooliganism. With the WHO's line of thought with regards to video games, that would mean the fact that we have a few football hooligans means football encourages violence, and we need to step in and brand that a disorder. There are probably more football hooligans out there than there are people who suffer from clinically classified mental health disorders in relation to video games. One in three people in the world identify as being interested in video games, and how many of those people, as per the World Health Organisation's classification, are in fact addicted to games?

'If I look back at my own upbringing, you could easily classify that as an addiction,' he adds. 'It all begs the question: where do you draw the line between an interest, a passion and an addiction? When I was younger, I might play video games for 12 or 13 hours per day. I was really lucky to have a parent who was supportive of my hobby in my mum. She realised from an early age that football, for example, wasn't my thing because I was quite a frail individual, I was quite small and skinny compared to my brothers. I just didn't have the stamina or strength to go out and play football and most other sports.

'I started collecting games, I started reading about them, I became consumed by the way in a way that I'd never have described as negative. From the outside looking in, I'm sure someone would be keen to label that an addiction against the WHO's latest inter-pretation, but in actual fact this was a passion that was monitored, looked after closely and encouraged by my mum.

'From a personal perspective, I had a very tough upbringing. My father was in jail at one point. I've not shared that with anyone. I lived in a really small community, where we had no support from friends or family besides my single mum. My means of escape at that time – against a background of poverty, of people taking drugs, crime, all of which is common in a working class environment – was video games. I couldn't afford to go out there and live in these natural environments, so game worlds offered me that portal to live in these worlds.

'I find the WHO's own findings patronising and quite damaging to suggest the opposite end of the spectrum is true, especially when they've not sat down and spoken to the individuals that have been literally raised by them, and have developed careers from them. Video games kept me away from drugs, alcohol, crime, all sorts of things that were going on in the background of my life in my formative years, and I can't imagine where I'd be now if it wasn't for that reprieve from reality they allowed.'

From a personal point of view, many of us have lived the benefits of games and have an instinct to fight this negative conception of something so dear to us, and so I empathise wholly with the idea that the WHO's classification excludes the tangible positives and the reality for millions of us out there who owe their life to video games. There's no disputing, however, that there are a small per centage who do demonstrate particularly addictive tendencies towards video games, and they need support, and so there are other considerations at play with this categorisation that are often missed in this discussion, as Dr Sachin Shah of charity Gaming The Mind points out.

The classification was something the WHO likely had to do, he believes, because the International Classification of Diseases isn't regularly updated and, as we've seen with loot boxes, opinion shifts between countries on where the line is on gaming's intersection with different facets of addiction. It also offers an important opportunity.

'The World Health Organisation has a global panel of clinicians and health care experts,' Shah notes, explaining that as a number of countries are worried about it, they will push harder for its inclusion. The issue isn't in the classification itself but how that is understood and interpreted beyond the broad stroke idea of games being inherently harmful. 'It's all well and good that they've identified it and named it, but that has to come with a lot of education alongside it. What it shouldn't be is a warning shot to parents. It shouldn't be: *okay, your kid is playing so much on the PC up in their bedroom, and this could be a disorder.* That's no more valid that saying your kid is sad and that could be a disorder of some sorts. It has to be done responsibly and people have to be aware that Gaming Disorder as it is described is likely to be very, very rare.

'There are, however, people in the world who do have problems related to playing video games too much to the detriment of work or life or school or money or relationships, and they keep on playing anyway. It's good to give it a name.

Don't get me wrong, there may be something else at play as well – we see that with depression, anxiety, social anxiety, ADHD, there are often elements which overlap in these conditions – but it's useful to have that language. If there's something you're suffering with, it's helpful to know that you can go and get help for it.'

It is this accessible language which might in fact open up the discussion of Gaming Disorder rather than close it down. We ask: would my passion for games be considered addiction? But what about those who worry the opposite, that their passion might truly be an addiction, unsure of how to articulate it or worried it might sound silly or not serious enough.

This clear medical classification gives an opportunity for people to seek help with a named concern and, as Dr Shah tells me, this might be vital in a number of countries to access the treatment. It's something I hadn't properly considered before our conversation: in my home of Scotland, it's easy to take the NHS for granted, but in America, for example, where access to healthcare is far from straightforward or cheap, seeking treatment for a condition that in essence doesn't exist may feel outright impossible.

NHS England has taken a firm approach, opening their national clinic aiming to address game addiction at the end of 2019. As part of the National Centre for Behavioural Addictions – which also supports internet addiction – it offers help to children and young adults aged 13-25 whose 'lives are being wrecked by severe or complex behavioural issues, associated with gaming, gambling and social media'.

'Health needs are constantly changing which is why the NHS must never stand still,' explains NHS chief executive Simon Stevens in the clinic announcement. 'This new service is a response to an emerging problem, part of the increasing pressures that children and young people are exposed to these days.' He did, however, second Claire Murdoch's call that it cannot be left solely to the NHS, noting companies have a responsibility to 'prevent rather than cash in' on obsessive and harmful behaviour that could be associated with their product.[7] The clinic cites WHO's classification as a driving force for addressing gaming addiction in their work, and is a clear example of how the classification can proactively take steps to support those whose behaviours align with those outlined as gaming disorder. While the clinic is in its early days, their work will contribute to our developing understanding of the issue at hand and offer support for years to come. It's arguable that any resources being secured to support mental health and wellbeing is a good thing, and, though many remain undecided on the disorder itself, a number of young people will benefit from the psychiatrists and clinical psychologists.

Dr Ali is part of a number of WhatsApp groups with parents and other teachers, many sharing the latest scare story about video games, and he feels the need to constantly counter their arguments that are accepted at face value.

And that's what scares me most about the classification and its lack of clarity: in the round-the-clock news, social media age, the average person is bombarded with headlines all day. They may tune the particularly sensationalist ones out, they may not, but what about when the concern is being raised by the World Health Organisation? Even the most rational news consumer would take heed. The idea of Gaming Disorder can be seen as a blanket condemnation for what could be passion or investment, and the disagreements span all areas from gaming, health to governmental. So, we need to ensure that resources are available and people are able to dig beneath the surface to understand exactly what this is and what it refers to, lest we lose a new generation of potential gamers, shielded from a virtual world that is seen as a threat to some, but could actually be their own escape, or passion for many others.

★ ★ ★

'Won't somebody please think of the children!' yelled Helen Lovejoy on the Simpsons many years ago. That's where my mind goes on my final concern: in its most stringently opposing stances, thinking of the children can be seen as shielding them from the potential danger of gaming's influence, or it's thinking of them so they don't miss out on what could be anything from a fun pastime to a lifeline in trying times. By the time this book goes to print, my daughter, Lily May, will be one-and-a-half, and I've already got her button-bashing her way through *Sonic Mania's* opening Greenhill Zone chapter. I hope to impart my knowledge of and enthusiasm for video games as she grows up and will likewise aim to underline the importance of balance in escaping into virtual worlds, and spending time socialising in reality.

For others less interested in video games or up to date on the bigger conversations around the topic, the WHO's classification might be all it takes for parents to prevent their kids from discovering the latest action-adventure game, Japanese role-player or MMO. In doing so, not only could that child lose the chance to discover new worlds and social experiences online, they could miss out on the chance of making new friends, and bonding more with those they already know.

'Before I fell out of football, one of the things I always wanted was for my dad to play with me,' says Dr Ali. 'That's an integral part of any parenting situation, the bonding experience. Nothing compares to that – spending time with your child, learning and experiencing one of their interests.

'One of the best bonding exercises I have with my kids is playing video games, because we're constantly learning at the same time. Like most parents, I sit down with my kids with their homework, but, equally, I use video games in our leisure time to teach them new things. That's not even considering the three-dimensional, persuasive and interactive nature of video games – no other medium lets you teach programming hands-on, or art, or sound, or gameplay. For me, nothing beats sitting down and playing video games with your children, nieces, nephews, friends, whoever and asking: What does the player need and what are they learning? What sort of environments are they most interested in, and what do they want to get out of their time inside these game worlds?

'Video games are unique in the sense that they facilitate a two-way conversation. You can talk about what you're doing at the same time, you can talk to each other through certain parts of games, you can interact – and you can do this in-person or online with other people all over the world.

'A lot of parents do see video games as a bonding opportunity, to be fair, and we're starting to see more and more parents sharing their stories of being able to bond with their kids via video games. I remember my daughter was asked to design a Halloween card at school, and she drew one of the characters from *Destiny* on there. I think that's brilliant! The characters from *Destiny* are great examples of interesting character design, and the fact that she's identified that and decided to use it in an educational context is wonderful. There's no onus on parents to sit down and play games themselves, but I do think they should, at the very least, learn what their kids are doing and understand the benefits – at both ends – that are to be gleaned from the experience.

'On a more superficial level, there was a really scenic area my kids were playing in *The Witcher 3* that I noticed looked similar to a park nearby where we live. I told my kids about it, we visited it that weekend and suddenly this virtual world is brought to life by somewhere they can identify in reality. For me, that's so enriching.'

As a parent of two teenage adolescent boys, Emma Kenny – This Morning's resident psychologist – shares Dr Ali's outlook on sharing gaming experiences with her children. By playing *Fortnite* with her kids, she not only understands the game, but has now grown to love it.

Kenny is dubious over the World Health Organisation's Gaming Disorder disease classification. Opiates, gambling or alcohol addiction – which can have 'a real devastating, profound impact on the life of the addict and of the lives of those around them', where she wonders if the conversation around video games and addiction in young people is in fact something different, being mistaken or disguised as addiction.

'I don't feel that any child can self-regulate – of course they can't, they're children,' she elaborates. Adults can take time to self-regulate and don't always manage it at all. Ultimately, children like doing things that they enjoy. If a parent doesn't manage that level of enjoyment, by altering the options available to them, then they'll do the thing that gives them the most feedback that's positive.

'I worry about the term "addiction" in this instance. I know that it's been taken on by the World Health Organisation, and I know that there are now addiction centres for gaming. If I'm being honest, I don't fully understand why we're putting it in that category. I think that anything I can unplug, and then go for a walk with my kid where they're not dealing with any withdrawal – because that's the issue with addiction, it's the context of withdrawal – isn't an addiction. I'm yet to meet a child who's been managed appropriately who has also had any negative withdrawal symptoms.

'I think we're medicalising an issue that's actually more about our failures as a community, and that, actually, we should probably take a bit more responsibility instead of saying, well, that's an addiction therefore we're helpless to deal with it.'

Naming *Fortnite* as a pertinent example, Kenny notes long spells spent within Epic Games' sandbox are long spells spent socialising – where players might engage in playful battles in the game's *Battle Royale* variant, or where they might build their own worlds and battle arenas together in its *Fortnite Creative* offshoot.

The idea that some adults struggle with self-regulation isn't unreasonable, therefore neither is the fact some could struggle to enforce similar restraint on their children. To exclusively and excessively engage in anything is likely to be detrimental but argues Kenny that to villainise something without proper consideration, is a dangerous process. Again, we come back to giving topics their proper scrutiny.

'The kids are gaining so much productivity from it that of course they're going to want to continually do it,' she adds. 'On a mental health level, as long as those kids are being managed appropriately – and that's the job of the parents – then I think the positives of playing video games far outweigh the negatives.

'Marketing-wise, Epic Games are very clever. Of course, they're working on the brain, making players want to come back and play more. That's how you make a successful anything, that's the way the world is. But, again, to villainise it is almost to say: as parents, we're not responsible for parenting our children. Secondly, that there are no good things about it, which would be intensely unfair, and also, I think, quite dangerous because there are kids who are disabled, there are kids living in the middle of nowhere, there are kids who really don't have a social network, and suddenly they've got a world that comes alive. People of a certain age might not understand it, but it certainly exists.

'As a parent, the main thing about any kind of activity is: if you're going to let your children do it, then you better bloody understand it! I don't really have a lot of patience for parents who moan about things and then have no clue when asked what they think about the thing they dislike. You shouldn't let your children on social media unless you know what that social media is. Doing so lets you be a presence within that dynamic, it lets you communicate. I always monitored both of my kids' social media use, until my oldest turned 16. He's 17 now and he can do what he wants, but in terms of prior rules and regulations – I could spot-check phones, I could minimise the amount of time they're allowed on the PlayStation, I could consistently manage how much time they're spending inside by actually taking them outside. That's all within my reach and remit.'

Kenny suggests that when this process breaks down it's because there's been a failing in parenting standards – which is totally okay, she says, as everyone screws up from time to time, in life, in work, and as parents or guardians. For her, owning your shortcomings is key, as opposed to placing sole blame on external factors like video games, which is in her eyes symptomatic of a blame culture we see often. Kenny reckons this is reductive and goes as far as to say levying blame at IT – the cyberworld and video games – is in turn, denying our future.

If we blame anything other than our own skills, in terms of managing children's time and engagement with gaming, we also deny ourselves power. If we deny ourselves power, then we feel completely out of control and helpless. If we feel helpless then our children won't be able to negotiate a normal balance, because they look to us as parents to be able to negotiate that and to be strong.

Kenny argues that subculture is also a huge part of the conversation that's often being ignored and that subculture plays a vital part within both video games and mental health. If people feel like they're on the outskirts of society, if they feel other or atypical, then it's not uncommon for their mental health to be affected. Video games allow those people to feel part of something bigger, to feel understood and feel like they belong.

'As simple as it sounds, another virtue of playing *Fortnite* is that people have a laugh. I hear laughter from my kids' rooms every single time the boys are on it. My boy started sharing his gaming stuff on Instagram not too long ago and he's got tens of thousands of followers now because he interacts with people, they interact with him, and it's fun.

'The wider participation now is incredible. My kids are playing with people in South Africa, who are playing with people in America, who are playing with people in Asia. The transactions and experiences they have now are not isolated. If we want to talk about isolation and the impact on mental health, then, of course, the worst thing for any human being is isolation with no socialisation. These days, video games are not isolation, they are connection. It's a blind connection, but you're still forced as players to interact with people via avatars and over headsets.

'Interaction is something that makes us happy and healthy. The skills that players are learning while playing these games can be and are being translated into the real-world and real-life. I also think there's a real democracy about the cyber world. For example, a child with autism, who might struggle with interaction in present situations, can now go online, natter away with people they might never meet, and actually enjoy a really interactive and connected experience. Those types of democracy elements in computer games is something that people are misreading.'

There is often a dichotomy in non-gaming parents' view of computers and technology: they will use and praise the good it does in the world, while using similar points as examples of perceived failings when it comes to video games. 'Ultimately, this idea that the gaming community is full of strange people who don't leave their rooms who're near-suicidal is massively disrespectful and completely unrealistic! Why are we pedalling something like that? We need to be very careful. We've got solicitors, barristers, doctors, high-level people, footballers, all of them, all gaming, all very successful… it's a story that's got the wrong narrative.'

It is more complex than asking 'Are computers good or bad?' There is scope for a nuanced debate around the pros and cons of technology in specific circumstance, lest we switch off our screens entirely, or, at the other end of the spectrum, wind up on the front lines battling an army of Skynet T-800 Prototypes.

When I worry for future generations of gamers missing out on what I and many others have had through fear that arises in the genre, I always have glimmers of hope. Video games and mental health charity Safe In Our World asks parents to Get Smart About P.L.A.Y in association with the UK Interactive Entertainment Association, focussing in on parental involvement, which can help with time spent in game, and potential spending. Their campaign encourages parents and carers to use tools to manager screen time, and in-game purchases in video games. Fronted by ex-professional football player Rio Ferdinand, the initiative follows a recent report from Europe's video game industry body which found that only one in five parents of children who spend money on video games use the family controls available on gaming devices. This is backed up by a 2019 NSPCC study that revealed just 19 per cent of parents of children aged 5-15 use family controls on internet-connected devices.[8] Given everything considered so far, Safe In Our World's campaign has scope to (re)invite parents into the fold to learn more about video games and be better informed to make their own judgements regarding online play and screen time.

I admittedly still have my concerns about Gaming Disorder as a medical classification, but there remains people on each side of every question here who – ultimately, when you dig down – want the best for people. Is that to shield them from the potential danger of games? Is that to highlight the wonder waiting within these digital worlds? We're still a long way from everyone being anywhere near on the same page on how that looks in practice, but it keeps coming back to seeking that nuance: looking beyond the broad stroke interpretations to see the benefits that games hold, understanding that the classification may cause stigma around gaming but it also might offer opportunity for treatment for someone who needs it. Even if you don't, diving deeper into the areas we don't understand to best support a curious mind for children in games to be creative and explore. We know mental health, addiction, and even Gaming Disorder are far from black and white issues with a cookie cutter solution, so as we go forward, all I can hope is that we take the time to really navigate the grey with an open mind, without villainising a form that can help many.

With that in mind, the campaign from Safe In Our World really strikes a chord with me. I can't imagine how different so much of my life would have been, had my own parents taken a dim view of video games and their beneficial qualities. Don't get me wrong, I'm sure I did their head in during my younger years, rabbiting on about finally beating the final boss in the first *Tomb Raider*, or winning La Coupe de Monde in *FIFA: Road to World Cup '98* with a depleted squad. We probably fell out once or twice when I'd promised to put the light out at 10pm, but was still playing *Resident Evil 2* at midnight, or when I came to Christmas dinner an hour late in 2012, because I just could not put down *Uncharted 2*. But, all told, they were cool, and for that I'm grateful.

CHAPTER 7

NIGHTMARES COME AND GO

DESIGN & OCD

My mum keeps a cracking photograph of my uncle Jim by her computer desk at home. Before embarking on his ill-fated property development career, my uncle worked as a cruise line casino croupier. Taken in one ship's sleeping quarters, the monochrome snap showcases a handsome man with messy dark brown hair, dressed in a pristine white shirt, two its two top buttons undone, and a pair of pressed black suit trousers. Jim is reclined on a chair, legs slightly wider than shoulder-width before him, hands clasped on his lap. Wherever he is in the world – my mum reckons the photo was taken in the early '90s, therefore somewhere between New Orleans and the Eastern Caribbean – he looks happy. He looks cool as hell too, sporting a pair of dark Ray-Bans, channelling his inner Mr

Pink or Blonde or Blue. Behind him is his bunk and behind that is a shelf housing his belongings. Given the transitory nature of the job, his possessions don't amount to much, and a lot of his shelf space is commandeered by a stereo surrounded by mountains of compact discs and cassette tapes.

I love this photo and yet there's a chilling irony to it all. Towards the end, Jim had accrued debt, similar to some of the folk he'd have dealt cards to on the casino floors. Part of his job entailed filling show homes with material goods, far more than he'd ever needed himself on the water. Towards the end, life was not sunglasses, immaculate shirts and smart trousers. It wasn't jet black hair and pearly smiles. Life was not luxury, mixing with holidaymaking revellers, or being slipped tips from winning high rollers. It wasn't music. It was avoiding debt collectors and being sent red letters from increasingly impatient banks. It *was* barely getting by; premature stress-induced greys, and Diazepam.

Every time I look at that photo, I allow myself to enjoy Jim's happiness. I choose not to focus on the life he lived years later and the hardship and hopelessness that eventually swallowed him. I think about what preceded this snapshot in time. I imagine him finishing one particularly long shift, hunkering down on that chair and deciding he'd look cool as fuck if he posed, Bond villain-esque, wearing sunglasses indoors. I wonder how long he'd known my auntie Vivian by this point – they met on the cruise liner circuit and wed in late '95 – who's at the opposite end of the camera.

I think about all of this until I don't. Because when I stop thinking about this, I start thinking about the horror of May 12,

2008. I think about the husk of a flat in Bath Street in Portobello. The apartment that instead of mirroring the two fully furnished properties above, sat unfinished and untouched until Jim's life insurance policy paid out. I think of the exposed joist in the back room. I think about Jim, sulking around on the day of his death and ultimately hanging from that very beam. His eyes wide, his face red, then blue, then purple. His hands thrash, the rope is taught, the wood creaks, his feet swing to and fro. He struggles, he regrets, he tilts a few degrees each way. Back and forth.

My mind obsesses over this dark imagery that I've conjured for myself. Before he died, I last saw Jim during the Christmas break of 2007. The next time I saw him was in his coffin at his funeral on May 21 – incidentally my mum's birthday. I didn't see him on the day of his death and yet have created a vivid picture in my mind of how he died, down to the colour of shoes he was wearing. It's amazing how the darker part of the mind works. Several years into a programme of anti-anxiety and anti-depression medication, I'm much better at managing it, but it's still something that presents itself over and over and over in my mind all the same. To this day, I struggle to control these thoughts as they come, but over time, and in concert with monitored Citalopram usage, I've become desensitised to the imagery; to the point where it's almost cartoonish, a caricature of a coping mechanism. Seeing the pictures I've normalised in my head for years written down on a page for the first time reminds me of how brutal, but also how absurd, these brain projections are. For long enough, I kept them to myself. I wasn't ashamed of them but I was definitely a wee bit embarrassed because it felt like an adult version of an imagination run wild. Instead of imaginary pals of dragons and cowboys and talking toy soldiers, I had Oor Jim, perpetually swinging from the ceiling. Which is hardly pub-friendly chat, is it?

* * *

By early 2015, I was in my final year at university, studying for a degree in journalism. Video games had always been a huge part of my life, and as an only child this worked well with being comfortable in my own company. What I lacked in human companionship, I made up for in virtual adventure, and I never once had to answer to anyone for hogging the joypad. I'd grown up chasing Chaos Emeralds in *Sonic the Hedgehog*, plundering ancient crypts with Lara Croft in *Tomb Raider*, and stalking undead zombies in *Resident Evil*. I'd won the World Cup with Scotland in *FIFA* (a tall order, I know), led Celtic to UEFA Champions League glory in *Pro Evolution Soccer* (we can but dream), and had built the biggest and most lucrative fairgrounds in Bullfrog's classic management simulator *Theme Park*. I credit *Lemmings* as the first video game I ever played – from then Dundee-based developer DMA Design, who in 1997 launched a wee game called *Grand Theft Auto*, and by 2001 moved to Edinburgh under the infamous Rockstar North moniker – and I can still name all 108 playable characters from Konami's 1997 Japanese role-playing game *Suikoden*.

I loved, and still love, all of these games. But it wasn't until playing games like *Depression Quest, Actual Sunlight* and *Papo &*

Yo, that I felt compelled to share the themes, goals and messages I'd found in my happily self-imposed isolation with people outside of my immediate circle. I learned from these games, grieved with them, related to them – and if I could do that then, surely, I wasn't alone? Yes, I'd sought escapism in action-heavy games like *BioShock*, but these games were designed by creators going through similar ordeals, tackling stigmatised themes head-on, and doing so insightfully and unapologetically. Even if I couldn't convince other people to play them – how do you recommend games whose protagonists are hopeless and potentially suicidal? – by writing about them, I could show people that video games are a vital storytelling tool, capable of relaying information like no other. I could show people that I'd had my own struggles with mental health, video games were a crucial part of pushing me to seek professional help, and that whether you're into video games or not, if you've ever felt the same, you now know you're not alone.

Given these personal goals, I wanted to reach out to Matt Gilgenbach, an independent game developer who has lived with Obsessive Compulsive Disorder (OCD) for most of his life. As a means of illustrating the darkest side of his condition – namely unsettling imagery of self-harm – his 2014 video game *Neverending Nightmares* employs a distinct comic book style aesthetic, whose grainy, monochromatic animations set the perfect scene. I don't have OCD but on first playing Gilgenbach's game, its portrayals somehow felt familiar. Disturbing visualisations are central to the game's makeup and I soon realised that not only was visualising uncomfortable imagery a means of dealing with grief and unpleasant situations, this was a video game dedicated to that very process. In doing so, *Neverending Nightmares'* sketchy, hand-drawn shadows guard its borders to create an inescapable sense of confinement. Its splashes of colour, which dance their way into certain frames – stained glass windows, orange candlelight, radiant pink pocket flowers, streams of crimson blood – which serve to accentuate the perpetual darkness beyond, and the evils that almost always lie within.

Gilgenbach had spoken openly about his OCD in the past, but *Neverending Nightmares* leads players through the complexities of how his condition affects him first-hand by making them wander the game's abstract spaces and confront the images as they relate to its narrative. In essence, Gilgenbach's own personal and depressive tendencies are reflected in the game's aesthetic, as it holds a mirror to mental illness by creating demonic manifestations of his innermost feelings. As the player delves deeper into *Neverending Nightmares'* plot, the metaphorical monsters that protagonist Thomas Smith face, get progressively more terrifying.

Smith is eventually seen self-harming and while it's removed largely from reality through the game's animated style, it is still harrowing to witness. Gilgenbach explains that this approach is owed to his desire to create something true to his experiences while also capturing a bleak, oppressive mood inside a world constantly closing in on the player. *Neverending Nightmares'* art style can be enjoyed without this prior knowledge on a superficial level – it is wonderful – and with a deeper level of appreciation. Equally, approaching the game's art style with such little restraint has not only helped Gilgenbach address his own feelings, but has also helped initiate a discourse around mental health within the game's community forums. Here players have interpreted the game's imagery against their own experiences and discussed how well-placed video games are to take on and deconstruct such complex themes.

Neverending Nightmares was Matt Gilgenbach's last roll of the dice on his journey to becoming a successful video game developer. Two years prior, he released *Retro/Grade* – a rhythm-meets-shooter title that sought to harness the enthusiasm once held for other popular rhythm video games, such as *Guitar Hero*. Gilgenbach reasoned that fans would already own the plastic guitar-shaped controller that shipped with *Guitar Hero* and therefore help his game, appealing to those familiar with the genre while also standing out through its shooter game features.

What sounded good on paper was difficult to execute. Developing video games is an onerous task at the best of times, but when you fold indecision into the environment – a direct result of Gilgenbach's OCD – the process becomes more daunting still. *Retro/Grade* became a critical darling but bombed commercially. By Gilgenbach's own admission he was too picky about every minor detail, which meant the game was delayed and its development process prolonged to the point where it missed its window of opportunity, so far as interest in rhythm games was concerned.

Gilgenbach says he was 'terrified' when it came to finally releasing the game into the wild, and for good reason; it bankrupted him financially, emotionally, physically and mentally. He sunk around £45,000 of his own money into *Retro/Grade*'s development, forking out for artists and attending expensive industry events in a bid to promote his passion project around the world. He had borrowed more cash on top of that from his parents. He didn't take a paycheque for four years. As if rubbing salt in the wound, he struggled to reconcile that while critics appeared to love the game, receiving top scores across the board, no one was buying it. Gilgenbach was ready to quit.

'I think I stole this quote from movies,' he ponders. 'But you never really finish a game, you just stop working on it.'

(Authorial interjection: can confirm this is true of almost all media, including books – nothing is finished until an impatient publisher prises it away from your clasped hands. Anyway…)

'There are so many things where you can deep dive and spend so much time getting every aspect of the characters or elements right. When I worked on *Retro/Grade*, I had to fight every fibre of my being from nit-picking on every little detail, yet I know I still frustrated my artists. Rather than saying, *Oh, you did a good job – I'm happy with the asset*, I had to instead say, *Okay, I don't care anymore, we've worked on this enough*. For them, it was difficult to hear me simply say, *Okay, no, I'm just washing my hands of it*. It wasn't a reflection on them, I thought they were doing a great job, I just got so consumed by every little thing that I wasn't happy with anything until I was exhausted.

'The whole thing made me consider quitting game development altogether. Independent game development is very challenging and it's very stressful, but it comes with great rewards. Perhaps not a ton of financial rewards – I don't think there are many indie game developers that are really making big bucks – but I think it's more about it being creatively fulfilling.'

Not long after the launch of *Retro/Grade,* Gilgenbach slipped into a possibly inevitable depression. He struggled to verbalise the thoughts and pictures in his head, and his pre-existing OCD got worse. In a bid to turn around how he was feeling, he turned to what he knew best: video games. *Retro/Grade* had scunnered him in more ways than one, but he was determined to have one more shot at video game success. But, what to make a video game about? The answer was simple, because it had consumed his entire life. *Neverending Nightmares,* a horror game that would depict the harsh realities of living with obsessive compulsive disorder, was born.

Swearing to do just about everything differently from how *Retro/Grade* was made, Gilgenbach formed his own independent outfit named Infinitap Games and set about forming a very fixed schedule and, crucially, a fixed budget. This time, he was far more aware of how his condition could impact his colleagues, and so generated a more workable working environment. Helped by a successful Kickstarter crowdfunding campaign, *Neverending Nightmares* would release on time and within budget. It was well-received by critics and players alike.

'With the perspective of time, I am really proud of what I did,' Gilgenbach continues. 'The amazing thing to me is that it's not really a game that you'd expect people would want to play. It's not fun, and it's deliberately frustrating and disempowering. So many games are about empowering the player, giving their choices and decisions gravitas, letting them do things they can't do in real life. With *Neverending Nightmares* on the other hand, we tried to do the opposite and make the player feel as powerless and helpless as possible. That's the opposite of normal game design. Because of what we did with the mood, the atmosphere, the themes – people were able to tap into that. They could come to a realisation that the game was worthy of their time and money even though it's an unpleasant way to spend a couple of hours.

'From a personal standpoint, it was very important for me to put the haunting imagery in the game, simply because it haunted me in real life. With my OCD, that imagery, those horrible depictions, they are such a big part of my experience. When I first decided to make my own horror game, I was very clear in my head that I didn't want to have it focus on gore and jump scares, and instead wanted to focus on the mood and the message, but I realised that was a disservice to myself and to portraying what I'd always felt accurately. For many years I was haunted by these extremely painful images. I thought it was the perfect opportunity to bring those experiences to light, share them, and say, *Look, this is what mental illness can be. This is what OCD can be, and it's really fucking scary!*'

Gilgenbach continues to receive feedback from players, myself included, impressed by how perfectly *Neverending Nightmare* represents their experiences. He's overwhelmed and forever grateful for the enduring conveyor belt of positive reactions, noting that despite feeling entirely alone during his lowest moments, these player observations prove it wasn't the case. He likewise feels that no one is ever truly alone, despite how mental illness can make those affected by it feel.

'I think a lot of people feel that alienation when struggling with mental illness and that made it less about me personally, and more about a collective of people having experienced things and relating to them while playing. The amazing thing is how much you can connect to the character. When you lose a life in *Super Mario Bros*, you say *I died*, you don't say *Mario died*. That was one of the things we felt was special about *Neverending Nightmares* – this was a story that could have been told in other ways, but the story could only be *experienced* via interactive entertainment. The interaction makes it an experience.'

By virtue of hindsight, Gilgenbach reflects on his *Retro/Grade* experience with relief, mostly because of the problems the whole ordeal impressed on his marriage. After pouring his heart and soul into video game he was once so sure would succeed, he was floored. He'd lost his money, his time and, something he now appreciates more than ever, the opportunity to bond with his wife. He met his future spouse Joanne during the development of *Retro/Grade,* at a time when the workload was calm in comparison to how it would eventually be. Shortly after he and his then-girlfriend started dating, he realised his rhythm-meets-shooter game was not doing as well as first thought, which meant he had to abandon pretty much everything on the peripheral of his life at the time, not least his social life, to focus on work.

'I thought that things were going okay and that I didn't need to overwork myself, until we started dating and then I realised how bad shape the project was in,' he admits. 'I had to push to get the game out there which inadvertently took years! During that time, we got married and it was such a strange experience being married to someone. I loved her, I knew she was right for me, but we hadn't had the time to properly enjoy the early stages of marriage.

'By the time *Retro/Grade* came out, we'd been married for two years and had dated for a year before that. It all seems so dumb in hindsight, but it was very much the case that I'd become so consumed with making this game that I didn't realise the sacrifices I was making. I was convinced that I had to make them, I had to finish the game, I had to be fully 100 per cent focused on what I was doing for work. It all tied into the obsessive compulsiveness that I struggle with, and I was unable to take a step back, take stock, gain perspective and realise that I should, you know, cut my losses. I knew the game was not going to be financially successful but I was in it too deep by that point. That's the thing I struggle with the most, with the virtue of that perspective. I'm still married today, with two kids, but I often think about the time I lost.

'Part of the reason I have reflected on this so much is because she told me that she'd made a ton of sacrifices for me and my game. She doesn't hold any of it against me, but likewise, I shouldn't take it for granted, that she did it for me. I think I was coming to that realisation on my own but it was eye-opening that she recognised that she wanted to be with me, warts and all – and there were a lot of warts in the earlier stages of our relationship. I just hope that I can make it up to her. I feel bad about it, because only with the benefit of perspective and time can I appreciate that the choices I was making were not good.

'Putting *Neverending Nightmares* into the world is something that makes me immensely proud. I'm hopeful it will continue to have a positive effect on its players and it'll continue to keep people talking and help remove the stigma around mental illness. It's a positive thing for the world and I'm really glad that I was able to accomplish that. We've since had other recognition in interesting forms – in Japan, for example, there's now a web-based manga that's inspired on the game's intellectual property. They released a number of issues and a whole story. I thought it was really great that people were inspired by the original idea and keen to explore it in a totally different manner.'

That scope for interpretation is one of the most wonderful things about *Neverending Nightmares*. Gilgenbach's breakthrough gem allowed me to revaluate the unpleasant images in my head, to break them down and to pull them apart. My mind still graphically wanders whenever I think of Jim, but I'm no longer scared of where it might go next. Instead, I feel empowered. I feel like the 30-something white-shirted man with the clasped hands, the sunglasses, looking fucking boss on a cruise liner docking in Caribbean shores.

Perspective in all of this is vital. Gilgenbach now well understands the sacrifices his partner made in their relationship's infancy, but I ask how his tumultuous professional and mental health journey has been perceived by his family, those that are closest to him.

'It's hard for people to accept,' he acknowledges. 'While my wife is familiar with everything involved in the process, *Neverending Nightmares* still surprised her. My sister was a big supporter of the game on Kickstarter right from the start, and yet she found some of it difficult to get her head around.

'For one, it's hard to see this person you know so well in that light, that they've experienced [self-harm], they've struggled with these thoughts. In many ways, this journey is harder for my family to make because they've known me my entire life. They can see the pain there and it's hard for them to see someone they love in so much pain.'

Throughout everything – the rollercoaster of emotions in game development, failure, building himself up again – Matt Gilgenbach is proud of his journey. It was one of discovery, cathartic release and enlightenment. And if anyone person or group of players can empathise or relation to his adventure, then all the better.

'We did something really special with *Neverending Nightmares*. I hope people can continue accessing the game for as long as technology allows. I also hope that people who haven't played the game get to experience it and learn from it down the line. Even the thought of that makes me so very proud.'

A NEW CHALLENGER APPEARS

PHILIPPA WARR

Philippa Warr is a specialist journalist I worked with at PC Gamer. *She's an esports expert, an enthusiast of quirky indie games, a dedicated* Animal Crossing *connoisseur, and a self-professed pop culture trash panda, whose writing has featured everywhere from* MTV *to the* BBC, *the* Huffington Post *and the* Guardian. *Pip is also a super talented illustrator, and is the pen behind the charming and adorable* Hum Hum *– an amiable humming bird who brings colour to the cheeks of everyday life.*

'I was 12 or 13 when I first realised my mental health wasn't right, so in some ways I don't remember my life without it hanging over me. All of my formative memories have come through that lens, whether that's through a good period or a bad period or a combination, it's never been absent. In terms of coping strategies, in the early years it was more whatever was mandated by the NHS, or by my parents. Because I was still a minor, I was still, technically, not making any of my own decisions. The only decision that I could make was not taking my meds and, of course, that wasn't the best idea.

'Given my age at that time, my mental health must have impacted my life in a way that other people must have taken notice of, as not being normal or 'typically teenage', as it were. I think we too often write behaviours off as people being moody teenagers; a quarter of a century ago, that would've been the tendency. While I can't remember exactly, I must have been doing something that was more than that or more extreme. I think one of the biggest things was the fact that I didn't feel anything, I just wanted to connect to anything. It wasn't that I was feeling down, per se, it was just feeling completely nothing.

'When I'm going through a good period, I find it very difficult to remember specifics about the bad period – it's that context-dependent memory. Then when I'm going through something bad, I find that I can't remember stuff that was good. Through this, I had to have different forms of counselling because that's what I was required to do in order to still be considered as proactive and doing everything I could to get better – that's how the UK health system works, most of the time. I had to go to art therapy, I had to go to a *really* odd counsellor, and it felt almost like hoop-jumping. You'd go, and you think it didn't feel right, but you'd persevere anyway. They'd ask things like, *Has there been any traumatic events in your childhood that you can remember?* and I'd have to say no because there weren't.

'So, I was like, *Okay, I guess I'll sit in this room with you for the next hour and… make some clay bricks and see what happens?*

I don't know, it was all very strange. It was a hodgepodge of very different things. My mum took me to a homeopathist for a while, who we stopped seeing eventually because she asked my mum to give up coffee and immediately said we were done with it! Joking aside, my parents really didn't know what to do so they were casting the net quite wide. A person that I knew, her mum was a hands-on healer, so in the spirit of trying everything, I learned reiki and now have a qualification in that. I don't use it because I don't really believe in it myself, which I think would feel dishonest.

'Over the years, I wouldn't say I actively, consciously sought video games for therapeutic reasons, but there are some games that I've thrown myself into. *Dota 2* (2013) is one of those games. *Animal Crossing: Pocket Camp* (2017) is another. I definitely tend to get a bit obsessive over something but it's often the case these things – video games, in both of those examples – offer just enough engagement that it keeps anxiety at bay, or it keeps damaging thoughts on the periphery. It tends to be things that are cyclical. In *Dota 2*, each game is generally 45 minutes to an hour long and goes through similar patterns each time. Rounds of *Dota 2* are social experiences too, so even if I'm not talking in them, I can trick myself into thinking I was still doing "friend things".

'In *Animal Crossing*, there's a daily cycle at its longest, but within that, it can take three hours for your fruit trees to regrow, for example, or it takes a few hours to get the next round of rewards. That stuff helps break life down into a manageable pace, I guess.

'What I noticed was that when I was writing about any of

this, I felt like I was taming something that was too wild or too unshareable. When I was writing, I don't think I necessarily realised how honest I was being in those moments. I was honest in that, the things that I wrote were my experiences, but there's always the realisation that anything you're writing is done for an audience. It's not this empty, abyssal, hopeless thing, because it has a form and a structure, and it's not a mess.

'Personally, I'm very cautious of what I put out there, though. I still share honestly, but I try to only share stuff that I'd be happy coming back at me. I wrote something quite personal for a website a few years ago about a particular game and it's the only piece of writing that I regret, because, retrospectively, it's not something I'm comfortable with having shared. I guess this is what any kid growing up with social media outlets like Instagram or Snapchat has to deal with on a daily basis. It's a case of, *What have I shared today that might come back to bite me on the backside tomorrow?*

'Like many others, I've often played video games as a means of escapism. I developed cubital tunnel syndrome, which is on the opposite side of carpal tunnel syndrome because I was playing games on my phone too much. You could look at that and say, *Yes, you're addicted to that game.* I'd argue that, no, I'm not addicted to the game, I'm addicted to taking a break from depression. In *Animal Crossing*, it's so moreish to have this thing where a nice animal tells me I did a good job. Rather, than, *Oh god, I've got a thousand unread emails in my inbox and the government wants me to do my tax return and I can't even get out of bed and get dressed.* These are very different things.

'*Subnautica* (2014) is definitely one of my favourite games for relaxing and zoning out from the real world, as is *Sea of Thieves*. That's where a bunch of my friends hang out who I'm okay with being more or less chatty with. I can happily just sit and fish with the friends that I play *Sea of Thieves* with. I play a lot of *Teamfight Tactics* as well, which is a *League of Legends* auto-chess spin-off. *Slime Rancher* was another big one for me because it's just so happy, but it was also designed in such a way that you could just tune out and do little loops of farming and investigating. *The Sims* and *Astroneer*, I love those as well – basically any sandbox-style game that lets me explore and do things at my own pace.

'*Forget Me Not: My Organic Garden* is a clicker game where you grow human organs, each of which has its own soul. It came out of a game jam in Japan. I got really into that for a while because it's an easy game to deal with, without too much stress. *Animal Crossing* is another huge favourite of mine, as is the *New York Times* crossword app for iPhone. I find that really helps me get to sleep, staring at a grid going, *Okay, cool, time to turn off the light*.

'Recently, I spent a bit of time playing *Ring Fit Adventure*, the exercising action-RPG game for the Nintendo Switch. I had a really bad depressive slump just after the New Year, no idea why, to the point I had to cancel a bunch of stuff, and basically be in bed and moving minimally under many, many blankets. Playing *Ring Fit Adventure* was something I managed to keep up during that time. It felt like I'd made it part of my routine, so the fact that playing it was feeding me rewards of new exercises and new levels and quests at just the right pace to keep me interested – that felt good.

'It's like, *Oh good, I'm doing one of those things that people wag on about*, where it's like, *You need to get endorphins*, and you're like, *yeah? Fuck off.* They're like, *Have you tried getting a runner's high?* And I'm like, *I've tried. It doesn't exist.* But, no, it felt good to get into that as it gave me a real sense of purpose, during a time where I felt a bit hopeless.'

CHAPTER 8

A DEEP DIVE

VIRTUAL REALITY & ANXIETY

I fucking hate networking. When I first decided to pursue a career in journalism, the thought of getting paid to write blew my mind. Until then, I'd made a living from bar work, labouring and plumbing – jobs that paid the bills, but none of which I particularly enjoyed. Repairing a burst pipe outdoors in the heart of January whilst watching your fingers freeze off isn't fun, neither is clearing a tenement building's choked communal drain, overflowing with soiled nappies and sanitary towels, in the sticky heat of summer. I still find it amusing that I can look back at that time in my life and say it was, at times, literally shite. *You always need a plumber,* was something I heard a lot back then. Which is true. Just don't call me.

I fucking love writing. Writing wasn't just a change of occupation, but a window into a new world, full of ideas and creativity and fulfilment. Better still, being allowed to write about video games, something I have always been so very passionate about, was a dream come true. Being able to write for reputable publications about how video games and mental health intersect filled me with pride and the more I wrote about both subjects together, the surer I was of my career change. In everything besides networking, of course.

I say networking, but what I really mean is socialising. Or rather, forced socialising. The anxiety I now take medication for is invariably tied to social situations. My mate Div and I share a running joke that if I ever go missing at a party, the first places to check are the four corners of the room. Sure enough, the gag played out as planned at his wedding last year because, come on, who really enjoys mixing at weddings? Worse still, who enjoys mixing at work events? I gave the latter some serious thought when I visited Rezzed, a video games expo, as a freelance writer for the first time in 2015. Open to the public and industry folk alike, it's actually really lovely; low-key and chilled out. Unlike some of the bigger, higher-profile gatherings – crammed with revellers and soundtracked by perfunctory heavy metal guitar music – Rezzed has a distinct focus on independent developers, which sees its show floors filled with less orthodox games and more projects which are particularly artistically creative.

Still, while walking around London's Tobacco Dock, I found myself a wee bit overwhelmed. So much of the video games journalism world unfolds online, so while spotting several faces I'd had Twitter conversations with yet had never met in person, the thought of actually introducing myself face-to-face felt absurd. At one point, I clocked Phil Savage – now *PC Gamer*'s UK editor-in-chief, then the magazine's deputy editor. A few years later, I'd sit two chairs down from Phil in Future Publishing's Bath headquarters after being hired as a full time staff writer at *PC Gamer*. Phil, myself and the rest of the *PCG* team would occasionally grab a pizza and a few beers, and I'd learn that Phil was a very lovely, very approachable man. But at Rezzed in 2015, my brain wouldn't allow me to approach him and say hello. Which, as someone who generally doesn't lack in confidence, is what makes social anxiety all the more perplexing.

While avoiding the lovely Phil and a number of other prominent video games writer peers at Rezzed, I happened upon another lovely man named Owen Harris. At the time, Harris was showcasing his then prototype video game project, *Deep* – a virtual reality (VR) game that used an Oculus Rift VR headset, headphones, and a custom-built self-calibrating belt that matched the player's breathing patterns with on-screen movements. *Deep* is, in essence, a digital version of a diaphragmatic exercise, whereby breathing deeply, a reticule in the centre of the screen expands and contracts to cause the player to ascend and descend respectively around a beautifully-rendered underwater expanse, full of magnificent cliffs and glittering coral.

Harris told me at the showcase that he'd had anxiety problems for as long as he could remember, and that it was after discovering deep belly breathing exercises that he felt inspired to transfer the basic theory and practice into a video game. Harris explained that the breathing techniques didn't cure his anxiety but did enough to make it more manageable, and that by adapting the methods in game form, he created his own little 'isolation tank' – then designed solely for himself. Harris eventually paired up with a Dutch artist named Niki Smit, who convinced him his project was worth pushing to the public.

At Rezzed, I experienced it for the first time and instantly fell in love. I felt so relaxed, so serene, and while I'd never even heard of deep breathing exercises at that point, I was instantly sold on the idea. While still in its prototype phase, Harris told me he'd turned to his own creation at the Game Developers Conference in San Francisco that year when he needed to destress following a string of intense meetings. Perhaps one of the most significant and touching tales of *Deep* in action at that time is one that was told by indie developer and mental health speaker Christos Reid. As I wrote for *VICE* shortly after my own experience with the game, Reid had once turned to *Deep* under similar mid-conference stress and was brought to tears by its effectiveness. Reid reckoned it had calmed him down more than anything else in his life. That, I could totally relate to. The moment I took Harris' headset and custom-built belt off, I felt several stone lighter. My head felt tingly in the same way you might feel after smoking a joint. I floated out of the booth and felt like I could take on and chat to the world. Furthermore, I was absolutely, *pos-i-tive-ly* certain I had to get my experience written down and the message out there.

I'm glad that I did because just over five years later, Harris has taken *Deep* further than I ever could have expected, and likewise received some well-deserved attention following the *VICE* article I penned singing the game's praises.

'It's been a crazy journey with this, and each part that unfolds is another surprise. That VICE article was a huge turning point for us, and we got a lot of attention after that. First of all, we started to travel more and more further afield. It's been to the USA, Mexico, Australia, India, Japan, all over Europe – we travelled with it a lot over the next year or two from there, to the point where it felt like we were getting on and off planes every other day. It was tiring, but it was exciting and fun as well.

'The other thing that happened, which was more important than the travelling, was that we were approached by a team of behavioural scientists who wanted to work with us. They'd been developing their own games and experiments for several years but were curious to see if they could initially form some measurements around *Deep* and what we were doing. They wanted to see how people felt before, during and after playing it. This was such a good connection, we had such a good rapport with those guys, the collaborations got deeper and deeper, to the point where they ended up becoming the core members of the team.

'We've been working with this team for the last several years, and, in fact, Joanneke did her PhD on *Deep* and tested it on hundreds of people – on teenagers with anxiety and depression, within special needs schools, a number of other educational settings and it's been great to watch *Deep* grow and evolve in that time.

'Joining up with these guys adds a degree of pressure, but it also adds a lot of support as well. It's great to be able to ask even the most innocuous questions. *What colour should this cave be? It should be this shade of purple. Okay, why? Oh, there's this study that suggests this colour helps people process X, Y or Z easier…* I'm oversimplifying but, seriously, having people there who know what they're talking about has been invaluable behind the scenes. It's great to have that level of insight on hand and to know that their input will absolutely help anyone who picks up the game is reassuring.

'Taking *Deep* in this clinical-based, empirical direction wasn't something I was necessarily ever expecting. Niki has a better head for that level of vision than I do. Initially, I said no to it. I was like, *No chance!* It seemed to be too much hassle than it was worth, to be honest, but it's been amazing.

'Being able to reach such a wide and a diverse number of players is wonderful. To be helpful in this world – that's a wonderful opportunity as well. We're still trying to figure out some pretty key stuff: we have all of our science stuff, the vision stuff, the manufacturer stuff sorted out now. The part of the puzzle we're trying to solve at the moment is to get the last bit of development funding that we need. We're *hoping* the project will be ready and finished in 2020 and then it'll be released in a home version that doesn't require the controller, and also a therapeutic version that does utilise the controller. I very much want both versions to be available to the public, but that might be with something that's controlled by the hands instead of by mapping your breathing.'

The more versatile *Deep* can be when it hits the public, the better. According to the WHO, 1 in 13 globally suffers from anxiety[1] and General Anxiety Disorders likewise count for as many as 30 – 35 per cent of the mental health problems seen by GPs in the US.[2] In Scotland, it's estimated that more than 1 in 3 people are affected by a mental health problem each year, with the most common illnesses being depression and anxiety. Moreover, one in three GP appointments relates to a mental health problem in Scotland, and it's understood that higher rates of mental illness apply to areas with higher levels of deprivation. About 1 in 8 Scottish people use an antidepressant every day.[3] And that's only the ones who are on record.

One of the most fulfilling things I've experienced as a writer is having close friends respond privately to my articles with their own mental health tales. Don't get me wrong, I'd rather no one suffered from bouts of poor mental health, friend or foe, but the statistics suggest that's impossible. Instead, I love that people feel comfortable enough to share how they feel in those darker moments – be that publicly or privately – in response to my own personal insights. Everything I hear continues to galvanise my belief that anyone who has struggled with anxiety should experience *Deep* at some point, whether or not they play video games, or are used to virtual reality exploration.

'The biggest obstacle for virtual reality to this day is that people are afraid of ghosts and murderers,' Harris points out. 'Nobody wants to come home at 9pm or 10pm and put a box on their heads. They're scared that doing so will leave them vulnerable to the murderers or the ghosts behind them. And that's a really hard thing to overcome.

'The two things we've been working on are *Deep* and gigantic data sets for breast cancer, which are two very specific applications. From a technology perspective, these wouldn't be possible through other means. I think virtual reality has so much potential in therapeutic application, creative applications, and productivity applications. Architects, 3D modellers, trades that like can thrive with VR – it amazes me that they're not working more in virtual reality already. It might just be that there's no big game yet. The scenario might be that we're in the pre-iPod moment of the MP3 player, or the pre-iPhone moment of the smartphone. What I'm most interested in, personally, is the Oculus Quest, the all-in-one VR headset. I'm horrified by Facebook, Oculus' owner, as a company and as such I'm really apprehensive to recommend this to people. It really bothers me that they have content up there around stabbing people, shooting people, and hitting people, but they don't have anything to do with touch or nudity or sexuality… because that would be obscene [in their eyes]. But that aside, I really do like the Quest. It's got everything right there. The stuff that I'm working on is so specialist that it's going to be fine either way, but I'd love to see the technology become more widely and readily available.'

Over the last ten years companies such as Oculus, Samsung, Amazon, Apple, Microsoft, Sony and Google have made significant strides in developing virtual and augmented reality hardware and there are now over 250 companies working on VR and AR-related products. Despite the seemingly huge potential of this market, only 11 per cent of America's population used VR every month in 2019, which, in straightforward terms, suggests folk aren't using it very often.

My main worry for niche video games like *Deep* is that they risk not being experienced to their full potential simply because the majority of video game players don't own, or have access to, the hardware required to run them. There's a clear difference between taking a punt on an obscure independent title at £15, as opposed to buying the latest console or a gaming PC at several hundred pounds in order to play one game. Not that commercial gain is Harris and his colleagues' primary focus, but I would love to see as many people get *Deep* into their living rooms as possible, so powerful and positive was my brief experience with its prototype. Over half a decade on, I wouldn't say I'm any better at networking, or cringe any less at the thought of it, but after my short blast of *Deep*, I was undoubtedly in a better headspace to grin and bear it.

'Given the inadvertent length of the timeline, it's remarkable that I am still as enthusiastic about the project as I am!' Harris muses. 'I fucking love that game. I fucking love it. I don't play it as much as I used to. But occasionally, if I'm really stressed out, getting it ready, fixing some bugs before it goes to show or something like that, I'll play it and realise... oh yes! This is fucking great! I love it. I really love it.

'I had a very bad year last year. I lost family members, I lost friends, I got divorced, and, Jesus, it's nice to have video games sometimes. Obviously, there can be dark sides to all of that as well, and you have to be mindful of the isolation things like that can lead us to. But, for the most part, it's great to be able to step out, to take a step back from all the bad stuff for an hour or two. To get away and ride your horse around in the forest. Or move these blocks around. Or *XCOM* some aliens. It's like anything, you can overdo your food, your pints, whatever, but it's all good in moderation.'

Today, I still fucking hate networking. I'm exponentially better at it now than I was back in 2015, sleuthing around the Rezzed expo show floor, avoiding eye contact like the plague and making sure I refrained from lingering too long in the same spot for fear of someone I knew striking up a pleasant conversation that my overriding anxiety would prevent me from enjoying. Mostly because I've learned to control my anxiety through medication and perseverance. Playing *Deep* taught me the virtues of breathing techniques, so while I still get the odd anxiety attack, I'm more aware of the signs that precede them – sweaty palms, a difficulty swallowing, slight loss of focus and a little buzz between my ears. I'm now better equipped to overcome them, which often involves grabbing a quiet corner, taking deep breaths and counting to ten.

I never did bump into Phil Savage from *PC Gamer* again that afternoon, but I did find myself wandering around the Rezzed show floor in a serene state, with a smile on my face, ready to chat and *almost* ready to network.

CHAPTER 9

36O-DEGREE THERAPY

VIRTUAL REALITY & PTSD

My paternal grandfather was killed at his work in 1971. Jimmy had worked in Glasgow's docklands for most of his life and was crushed against a wall by a colleague operating a forklift truck with an obstructed view. Having lost his mother at just six years old, Jimmy's fatal accident meant my dad had lost both parents by the age of 23. Jimmy had also served as a Commando – a Royal Marine, today's equivalent – in the Second World War. 'Anyone who says they weren't scared is a liar.' Like many serving veterans, my dad tells me that my granda didn't talk much about the war afterwards. It just wasn't done. It's probably no wonder, given some of the things Jimmy and his peers would have seen and done. I never had the chance to meet Jimmy, but the story goes that he and his squadron were deployed by parachuting from planes at night over enemy territory. During one firefight, he carried an injured colleague for miles over his shoulder to an extraction zone. On another occasion, part of his finger was blown off by shrapnel. Despite his bravery and suffering, he missed out on The Victoria Cross medal of valour. Couple this with how the Black and Tans' presence in Ireland was partly responsible for my grandmother Catherine's forced departure from her own country at the turn of the 20th century, I take a dim view of the British Armed Forces. But that's a conversation for a different time. Granda Jimmy's well-worn line on the matter: 'Those who talk about the war weren't there.'

This speaks to the horrors he and his mates would have witnessed, underscores the shut-off, British stiff upper lip attitude that's unchanged today, particularly among Scottish men. Back then, talking about pain and trauma just wasn't done to avoid showing weakness, emotion or, I imagine, fear itself. In 2014, 10 per cent of Scottish ex-serving veterans reported having mental health issues, 2 per cent of which had been previously diagnosed with post-traumatic stress disorder (PTSD).[1] Whenever my dad tells me stories of Jimmy throwing himself out of a plane into enemy territory, or the thought of him fighting, almost certainly murdering opposing soldiers in close quarters combat, I can't help but be reminded of deployment in the likes of *Fortnite* and *PlayerUnknown's Battlegrounds*, and firefighting in *Call of Duty* and *Battlefield*. That's not to oversimplify or diminish the significance of their experiences of facing war, but in many parts of the world the majority of us don't have hands-on, real-life experience in this area – surely a good thing.

With PTSD specifically in mind, the University of Southern California's Institute for Creative Technologies has spent three decades working those video game elements into clinical study with the help of virtual reality technology. If you're fond of video games and are old enough to remember the early and mid '90s, you'll likely remember when virtual reality first came to the fore and the subsequent premature hype. Then billed as a cutting edge, life evolving, earth-shattering 'transformative systems,'[2] VR was going to change the world as we knew it... before it was priced way beyond the average video game enthusiast's reach. You could play *Sonic* or *Super Mario* on the cheap, without a clunky headset that looked like a second-hand rear projection telly strapped to your head.

Despite its potential, virtual reality in theory and practicality had failed. Over the last decade, VR has returned to the mainstream's periphery, but even today, the jury is still out on its ability to deliver on those 30-year-old promises. For clinical application, on the other hand, the initial early '90s scope was enough to get the idea of VR-inspired treatment rehabilitation off the ground, sufficiently, though costly and difficult to create and modify.

Albert 'Skip' Rizzo is a veteran psychologist and the Director of Medical Virtual Reality at the University of Southern California's Institute for Creative Technologies is one such champion of the medium who researches the design, development and evaluation of virtual reality systems via clinical assessment, treatment rehabilitation and resilience. Although primarily focused on PTSD in relation to the military, he and his colleagues have addressed social skill training in people with autism; PTSD in relation to sexual trauma; cognitive tests in VR for kids with attention deficit disorder; and the development of game-based rehabilitation applications for people in the aftermath of a stroke or a traumatic brain or spinal cord injury, to name but a few.

Through this, Rizzo believes placing patients in relatable video game-like scenarios can be beneficial in helping them engage with treatment via a process called 'exposure therapy', where patients narrate their traumatic experiences as if they're happening in the present.

'Exposure therapy is an evidence-based treatment, which means that there's been sufficient scientific research to document its effectiveness, in its traditional format, using imagination,' Rizzo explains. 'The primary aim is to help a patient confront and reprocess difficult emotional memories surrounding their trauma, but in a safe place.'

Rizzo describes the process as a 'hard medicine for a hard problem', as it requires patients to not only face up to their trauma but to explore and relive something they've normally trained themselves to avoid. Therefore, exposure therapy is a method of engaging with and narrating personal trauma as 'anxiety-provoking', which is why the presence of a trained clinician is imperative. Repetition plays a huge part in all of this too, because as the patient digs deeper into their emotions time and time again, all going to plan, they will process and normalise any negative thoughts. This is known as extinction learning, whereby the patient has a physiological brain reaction.

'We're simply trying to help the patient reprocess the event. We want to ensure the patient is not constantly retriggering their event, that they're not restricting their engagement with everyday life. The challenge with all of this is that, via imagination, you're asking a patient to do what they've been trying to avoid for months, years or decades.'

By introducing virtual reality into the equation, the patient can be transported straight into these digital worlds that leverage audio, visual, vibration technology – with subwoofers and a platform – and even smell. If a patient drove a Humvee military truck in a war zone, for example, the vibrating platform can simulate the feeling of driving a heavy vehicle over bumpy terrain. If there was a bag of trash on the side of the road in one patient's memory, or a lot of pollution, or dead animals, those odours can all be replicated in-game. If a roadside bomb went off, the noise and feelings of that can be emulated as well.

Rizzo describes this as a 'four-level sensory experience', which clinicians can alter and manipulate on the fly as the patient works through their tailored worlds. The time of day within the memory can be tweaked as can the weather. At present, he and his colleagues have access to 14 different combat-related worlds to treat PTSD and seven sexual trauma-related ones.

Developer Maxis' city management series *SimCity* is a great example, in Rizzo's mind, of video game-like scenarios in relation to brain training, rather than repetitive clinical drills. He says this level of sustained immersion is particularly important when treating PTSD and VR has shown its potential for both physical injuries and mental health issues; its benefits can be plentiful.

'PTSD and anxiety disorders, like phobias, are characterised and propagated by avoidance,' Rizzo continues. 'When you avoid something in fear, or it makes you feel anxious, you get a temporary sense of relief, and that reinforces continued avoidance. The brain doesn't learn that was then, this is now, and things that are reminiscent of the trauma are no longer going to hurt you. You're in a safe environment.'

VR is essential to this process because, although evidence-based, exposure therapy is not an exact science and not everybody is good at visualising their circumstances and scenarios. Virtual reality can be essential to this process because it allows patients to be immersed in simulations of their trauma, at a gradual pace, to help them confront and process these difficult emotional memories and, crucially, move forward. War-based series such as *Call of Duty* or *Battlefield* might perpetuate a cathartic revenge fantasy, suggests Rizzo, but the idea is to get patients to deal with their anxiety by placing them in a context that resembles a hurtful scenario, but – it bears repeating – at a pace that they can handle.

In turn, graphic fidelity – how realistic the VR scenario is – plays a huge part in their therapy. Nowadays, the readily available technology can mirror reality pretty closely, but back in the mid-'90s visuals were blocky, rough-edged and crude. This poses a pretty key question: how real does virtual reality in a therapy-based situation need to be in order to work? It's one thing aspiring to the *Star Trek* Holodeck, but until that level of realism is possible, clinicians must work within the bounds of today's technical constraints.

'Our mantra was always diversity over detail,' Rizzo explains. 'To have a diverse set of environments was always more important to represent the nature of the individual's experience.'

This is where exposure therapy's broad range of trauma-related scenarios come into play, each of which transports patients to specific locations and moments in time. Even if the graphical fidelity of the simulation isn't of *Call of Duty*-level realism, the patient's brain will nevertheless react to the triggers around it. The literature and research available today proves that exposure therapy is improved when used in concert with virtual reality.

'The frontal lobe of the patient's brain knows that they're in a research space or clinical surrounding,' explains Rizzo. 'But the perceptual cues of the environment are sufficient to activate the fight or flight area of the brain, and the other areas that manage this fear response.'

So, the patient's brain reacts to the simulation as it were real life, even if they're well aware that they can remove their VR headset and be back in reality in an instant. Despite budget constraints at present, Rizzo is also of the view that so long as VR tech keeps improving and evolving, the price of powerful tech will continue to fall. Something else that's bigger and better might have taken its place in realism terms, but organisations such as the Institute for Creative Technologies will always rely on a trickle-down effect-style model. In their quest for higher-end graphical fidelity, Rizzo admits that re-traumatising will always be a concern in the process of treating PTSD, but this outcome hasn't been borne out of the research, it is now in its fourth decade of evolution. This is mostly down to the consistent one-to-one, checking-in process in the way therapy is administered by clinicians – wherein patients' anxiety levels are tracked, while being asked directly if they wish to continue pushing the simulation forward. Gradually, clinicians will ease patients into the process of reliving memories so as to avoid throwing them in at the deep end too quickly.

Avoiding something you're scared of, like seeking professional health for poor mental health, offers a temporary sense of relief, but it won't help in the long-term. Instead, avoidance reinforces continued avoidance. In the case of those who went to war like my granda, for example, this can lead to chronic PTSD. It's at this point that all of what Rizzo has said truly hits home hard for me.

'You might have a guy coming back from Afghanistan or Iraq, driving down the 405 Freeway in Los Angeles and he sees trash at the side of the road. All of sudden it triggers the memory of an improvised explosive device going off, hidden in the trash, instantly killing his best friend. Now, he doesn't want to drive.'

By relating the adverse effects of PTSD to day-to-day activities, it's easier to understand how ex-service members can struggle to reassimilate and readjust to life away from warzones. The thought of losing your best friend in such a tragic situation is horrific; in framing how this can filter down into every day, otherwise innocuous scenes – such as trash at the roadside – it gives a small insight into how overwhelming PTSD and its hidden triggers can be, especially for us who haven't experienced it.

The United States of America has seen a spike in the suicide rates of ex-service members in recent years, which has galvanised the Institute for Creative Technologies' work with those with PTSD. Support from charitable organisations is also at its peak and Rizzo singles out Soldier Strong – a charity who donates VR equipment to the Veterans Health Administration – for individual praise, and believes that every VA hospital will have access to virtual reality-driven exposure therapy in the not too distant future. The advent of affordable mobile headsets, such as Samsung's Gear VR, means there is scope to decentralise the process of mental health treatment, which consequentially could help it reach more people.

Research has explored if virtual reality therapy can boost feelings of self-compassion and reduce depressive symptoms. University College London and Catalan Institution for Research and Advanced Studies explored this in a 2016 paper, where their pilot study examined 15 adults aged 23 to 61 with depression. Via three weekly eight-minute sessions, the group used virtual reality headsets to see from the perspective of a life-sized avatar before being asked to express compassion towards a distressed child. Afterwards, the patients embodied the child and were made to listen to the adult avatar repeating their recorded words of compassion back. One month after that, nine patients reported reduced symptoms of depression, while four experienced 'a clinically significant drop in depression severity' following the therapy. Some patients also said they were less self-critical in real-life situations afterwards. Of course, this was not a large sample, and this particular study was conducted without a control group – but I feel it's worth singling out, simply because self-criticism is so often a central tenet of depression.

'Now we're all finally here, looking at VR running off a mobile phone and looking at high fidelity headsets like the Oculus or a Vive that blow away the head mounts of ten years ago, that cost tens of thousands of dollars,' considers Rizzo. 'When a clinician can open their desk drawer and use a headset like that, with no computer necessary, hand it to a patient with the scenario ready to play out, data from the interaction can be collected, and now you've got a tool that could be very adoptable by any clinician.

'We have to be careful because we're very fond of saying VR is an emotionally evocative technology, which we can use to activate emotions in people in ways that we can positively use in a therapeutic process. That's all great and we love that, but if you're going to accept that, you have to also accept that if you're going to make these environments available willy-nilly without the supervision of clinicians and experts, the whole thing can easily go south. When you're dealing with PTSD, this is not something a patient should attempt to self-diagnose. By all means, getting standalone headsets and treatment initiatives out there into more people's homes would be great, but only if done in conjunction with those who know what they're doing with it.'

Rizzo reckons public speaking apps are one of the few do-it-yourself treatment programmes he might advocate for, because they help us improve a day-to-day skill that most people have experienced at one point or other in their lives. Still, he does so with caution and admits stay-at-home therapy can be a slippery slope. AI treatment development muddies the waters further still, and even in his work the behaviour of virtual humans must be tempered and measured. Who knows when things will go full Judgment Day a la *Terminator 2*, but Rizzo believes we're approaching a time where virtual therapists will be proposed, which means we've got to be careful about putting programs out there that are doing more harm than good. To this end, AI, self-training and self-treatment programmes will be among the most contentious issues in clinical psychology, as Rizzo sees it, and the fact that all of these things will be readily accessible online makes the prospect just that bit more daunting.

'Think of Alexa but embodied in a way that's engaging, perhaps a virtual companion. Ultimately, what we want to avoid is replacing clinical care with software, when there isn't official validation.'

In doing so, not only do you risk doing harm, but you also run the risk of someone engaging with that software, not getting what they need, and then falsely assuming that they can't be helped. When I finally plucked up the courage to visit the GP, if I told him I was depressed and he said there's nothing he could do – I can't imagine where I would go next.

When I think about *Deep* and the instant reprieve it gave me from real-world anxiety and stress, it's easy to see how virtual reality-led exposure has the potential to help patients overcome mental hurdles. Had this been around in my granda's day, I don't know whether he would have been interested, but I'd like to think it could have helped those who faced some of the worst parts of humanity and felt unable or unwilling to talk about it.

Exploring virtual reality and how it can allow people to confront their fear through reliving a moment again and again isn't lost on me, either. If I could, I'd revisit the afternoon my dad told me about Jim's suicide. I'd normalise the entire ordeal

– an event that I've spent well over a decade building up in my head to the point of fable. I wouldn't linger downstairs, like I did in reality. I'd go straight up the stairs and give my mum the tightest hug, much quicker than I did the first time around.

A NEW CHALLENGER APPEARS

ASH SKYQUEEN

Ash is a prolific Grand Theft Auto V *YouTuber whose speciality involves recording videos of her in-game avatar performing death-defying skydiving stunts around the game's sprawling digital landscape. Otherwise known as Skyqueen, Ash is a big part of the performance subculture which exists in* GTAV *and first got involved in the in-game stunting scene when an injury prevented her from working. In real life, Ash suffers from vertigo and believes her extra-curricular endeavours in* Grand Theft Auto V*, as well as the online community, has helped her cope with her poor mental health.*

'I suffered a prolapsed disc in 2013 and it was just a wear and tear issue back then. I didn't realise at the time, but I think it started when I was around 18 years old. I had a spate of back pain issues, but it was something that I got over. I carried on after that, but eventually, after several years, it got to the point where I was getting a lot of unexplained pain. I'd taken some time off work, I'd been off for about three weeks, and one morning I stretched a little too far. The pain at that point was unreal I couldn't stand up at all and I was screaming in agony. I was sent straight to the hospital and found that the disc had completely worn away.

'Recovery time, at first diagnoses, was a big question mark. I was bedbound for about 18 months. At the 18 month mark I could get up but I still couldn't do anything as it was extremely painful to stand. I was still using crutches in 2016 and it was something that needed surgery to correct. Once they got the piece of debris out of the nerve root, it significantly improved things but the mobility issues are going to be here for life. I still can't hold a job to this day. I tried for three years to return to the old one as a security guard at the Metro Centre in Newcastle, which is a huge site that saw me walking upwards of ten miles per day. They did everything they could for me – looked at different roles, getting me off the floor, right down to just turning up every day on the lightest of duties where I was essentially not doing anything. Still, I only managed that for about a month and a half before I had to call it quits. I just couldn't handle the commute to and from work every day. I've now resorted to broke-ass YouTuber.

'I've always been into the *Grand Theft Auto* series, right from the very first one. I wouldn't have called myself a hardcore gamer, but playing video games was always something I was drawn to on my days off. My job involved working with a lot of people on a daily basis so when it came to downtime, I was most interested in being left alone. So, I'd play video games for large chunks of those two days I had off every week. Now I was stuck in bed or on the couch. I'd exhausted Netflix and everything else on cable TV is on repeat. I played *Grand Theft Auto V* to death when it first came out, I'd rinsed its single-player Story Mode, and had then reached that point where I felt like I'd seen it all.

'Then it was a case of *Okay, hang on, what's this "Online" button?* I'd never really played any online games before that point aside from a little bit of *Call of Duty* and even then I didn't really engage with other people. I'd never used a headset before to chat with other folk, or anything like that. *GTA Online* was the same at first, until I started to get involved with other players.

'It started slowly. A few people started inviting me to missions. A Scottish crew named the Tennent's Special Crew invited me in because I'd played in one of the missions that required four players. It was them that got me talking and engaging with more of the community, and ultimately, it was them that pushed me into YouTube as well.

'Video games, without a doubt, helped my mental health after the injury. The job I had to leave behind, I'd been in that since I was 19. I saw myself continuing in that career until retirement, I was quite happy on the site that I was on and the job that I was required to do. The money was good as well, so there was no reason to think about anything further on. The significance of the injury didn't properly sink in until about two years in, when I realised that this was something I wasn't going to just get over and get back to work. At that point, it didn't seem to have gotten any better, and, as hard as it was, I realised at that point that the best I could hope for, actually, was that it didn't get any worse. That, as you can probably imagine, brought up a lot of issues for me. I couldn't really do anything outside of the house. I have to plan ahead for absolutely everything that I do. If I'm going to go to the shop and pick up a few things, I know that it's going to impact me tomorrow. Balancing that, and at the same time worrying about how I was going to live if I couldn't earn a wage, wasn't nice at all.

'At this stage, I've completely given up on the benefits system. It was a constant fight to get support in any way. It'd take me three weeks to get in front of a doctor – and I could only see the doctor on a good day, otherwise I couldn't leave the house because I can't walk – and then you're trying to claim disability benefits from someone who's judging you when you're looking okay. Sure, I might have looked okay standing there on that given hour of that given day, but put me in a 9-to-5 job Monday to Friday and I know I'm only going to last a week or two, tops, before spending three months in bed. That's how bad the injury is, but it's hard to really show people that part after you walk out the door. When it comes to physical activity now, I just can't go past a certain point. I've had to adapt as best I can, I've had to find a way to cope with it. Trying to work through the benefits system was just making things worse, it was causing more stress dealing with the constant letters dropping through the door from the Department of Work and Pensions telling me they'd stopped my claim because I didn't attend an interview for a job that I knew I couldn't do.

'That does really impact my mental health for sure, but having *Grand Theft Auto V* there, and everything that comes with it – the YouTube side of it, the social elements – I wouldn't be able to cope if the game itself wasn't at the centre of everything, keeping me going and giving me something to look forward to away from everything else that was and is negative around me.

'I'd never heard of the stunting community in *GTA* before I started doing it. I'd maybe seen the occasional clip here and there, and I assumed it was Rockstar paying people to make the game look good. Before my injury, to be brutally honest, I didn't really use the internet. The internet to me was something that I had to use at work, very occasionally, when I had to send an email – or I would do a bit of shopping or pay some bills. I didn't even have a laptop until I decided that I wanted to record footage and play around with video editing.

'And I've never been on a plane! I'm terrified of heights! No way, I couldn't go near skydiving in real life. But I don't think the draw for me to do skydiving stunts in the game was ever because it's something that I can't do in real life. *GTA* doesn't trigger that phobia for me, which is another weird thing. I love mastering game mechanics and finding all the cheeky spots and the things most people don't expect.

'The fact that I can play this game however I choose, away from the heists and crime and murder, is the appeal for me. That's always been the appeal of *Grand Theft Auto*, even from the early games, the fact that you've got this open map that you can explore at your own will, at your own peril. You can choose when you want to do the missions if you want to do them at all. If you'd rather mess around and experiment with your surroundings, you can do that instead too. I used to ride motorbikes around in the early two-dimensional top-down versions, getting police chases around the map. It was one of the first games that I ever played that had that wonderful open structure to it.

'The whole performance and stunt culture have been waiting for *GTA VI* for three years already. We're just holding our breath for news on it to drop. It'll be as big, if not bigger than it was before. And I can't wait!'

CHAPTER 10

DRIVING ROUND
THE BEND

ROLE-PLAY & RESOLUTION

I find writing about my mental health cathartic. I use an area of interest to frame the conversation, which, more often than not, is video games. Cognitive behavioural therapy didn't click with me; instead, it's been a balance of medication and talking – most often via writing – that's helped me overcome my biggest demons.

For me, one of the most interesting and beautiful things about *Grand Theft Auto IV* was that I have taken solace in a game that was very much not even designed for this purpose. Realistically, the distraction *GTA IV* has offered me could have occurred in any online game. All I needed was friends, laughter and a virtual space to combine the two. What was very specific to the *Grand Theft Auto* universe and mental health are the following two stories I wrote for *VG24/7* and the *Guardian*'s video games section. Both were written in 2019 and covered *Grand Theft Auto V*'s role-playing on PC – a host of player-created online servers, independent of the official game, where users play by real-world rules, work jobs, host get-togethers and generally do not break the law. Through this, players are more open to conversation, and while most assume alter egos or portray make believe characters, some use the space to show vulnerability, and to discuss mental health and interpersonal subjects.

Both the *Guardian* and *VG24/7* have kindly allowed me to republish both stories in full here (in which those involved consented to be featured, with some names changed) which I feel illustrate the powerful crossover between video games and mental health through the lens of mainstream games – in this case, one within a series whose themes and motives have been heavily questioned since its inception in the late '90s.

★ ★ ★

CAN GRAND THEFT AUTO V HELP YOUR MENTAL HEALTH? YES, SAY ROLE-PLAYERS
Published by the Guardian – *Wednesday, May 1, 2019*

It isn't the tumbling, 360-degree views of San Andreas that command our undivided attention from the top of Mount Chiliad. Nor is it the whir of the cable cars. And it's not the blanket of mist that engulfs the valley below, nor the implacable sunrise that invades every inch of the towering cliffside's crevices and chasms.

At 2,619 feet above sea level, our group of five is hanging on Craig's every word, an unassuming *Grand Theft Auto V* role-player, as he shares a personal tale about his mother's alcoholism, how she was knocked down and killed as she left her local pub one evening and how he has struggled with depression and anxiety ever since.

Contrasting with the themes of virtual violence and crime associated with *Grand Theft Auto*, Craig is part of a group that uses the game's long-established but still ever-growing PC role-playing scene as a safe space for discussing mental health.

'My mother chose alcohol over her own wellbeing, and her family's, too. She had taken separation from my dad pretty bad and starting drinking a lot. My sister and I put it down to her way of dealing with the breakup, and, because she didn't appear to be drinking in the house or at work, we failed to notice it becoming a serious problem.'

Grand Theft Auto V launched on consoles in late 2013 and arrived on PC in April 2015. Role-play servers on the latter platform, where players act out characters of their own invention in-game, followed shortly after. Today, despite its age, the crime simulator's role-play scene is thriving. My mountaintop encounter with Craig and his friends takes place in one of FiveM's servers – a bustling 32-person open-source modification that lets users work, live and socialise by virtue of jobs, amenities and voice chat. Players are expected to live as they would in the real-world and obey laws that are enforced by voluntary police and emergency service role-players in turn.

Here, on this server, players enter Rockstar North's satirical swipe at modern America to try to pursue an honest in-game living, reflective of reality, that eschews the exaggerated chaos that is the open-world game's default state.

This isn't to say virtual crimes don't occur within the Los Santos role-play experience – far from it – but voice chat combined with a less crime-centred world provides scope for more nuanced encounters, such as the pseudo-self-help group I stumbled upon.

'I'll never forget the night we received the call,' said Craig. 'Mum had staggered out of the pub and was knocked down by a bus. She was pronounced dead at the scene, and that really triggered my own depression and anxiety. It's been three years and I've been to counselling, had cognitive behavioural therapy and now I'm on a course of antidepressants. I'm not 100 per cent, but I'm getting there.'

When we reach the foot of the mountain, I thank the group for letting me tag along, and Craig specifically, for sharing something so personal and sensitive. The group's members part ways but not before informing me they gather every few weeks for similar meetings and that I'd be more than welcome to join in again.

I take note of the group's individual player tags and agree to catch up soon. In a world designed to inspire theft, murder, drug dealing and general bad behaviour, there's something beautifully incongruous about what this group is doing in San Andreas, the game's imitative slant on Los Angeles, which serves to underscore the unconventional and idiosyncratic nature of the *Grand Theft Auto V* role-play scene.

Weeks pass before I spot Craig online again, this time with a few familiar and some less recognisable faces at Legion Square, the server's meeting hub. I'm welcomed warmly and we walk for a while with no obvious destination, eventually following the train tracks that run between the Port of Los Santos and Vespucci Beach. Along the way, a man named David openly discusses his real-life gambling problems.

It's all relayed within the guise of role-play, but David tells the group that at its worst, his addiction led him to money from his closest friends, and that his gambling spread to everything from football coupons to darts and horse racing, winnings from which he'd use to purchase Shark Cards – in-game money for *Grand Theft Auto* Online. As we circle back into town, the group commends David for having joined a Gamblers Anonymous group.

Later, a woman named Christine pulls up to Legion Square in a battered motorhome and suggests a camping trip to Vinewood Hills. Six of us set off, and with the sun setting over Blaine County and the stars now dancing over the Los Santos city skyline, Christine chats about drug use. Her brother-in-law had died by suicide a number of years ago, she tells us, and she's since spent much time stifling feelings of grief, loss and subsequent family dysfunction with recreational, drug-fuelled binges that temporarily help, but ultimately accentuate her suicidal thoughts.

Christine doesn't consider herself a drug addict but recognises she's doing more harm than good to her mental state and self-esteem. Like the others, Christine's admissions are raw, heartfelt and relatable.

Weeks later, I re-join the group at a house party-style get-together in an area of South Los Santos named Strawberry. There are more new faces, and as I work the room introducing myself, they chat about sports, video games, family pets and other interests.

After a while, Craig asks whether I fancy sharing anything personal of my own, and I oblige. I'm suddenly very aware of the intimacy forged by the compact setting, as the party-goers fall silent and turn their attention to me. I tell the group about my uncle's suicide in 2008 and the impact this had on my family and my mental health. I speak of how I went to Australia for a couple of years with my girlfriend to escape how I was feeling at the time, but that my depression and anxiety awaited me on my return.

I explain how it took me a year and a half to acknowledge the problem before visiting a doctor, and a further two years to pursue counselling and a course of medication.

While I believe that mental health issues should always be addressed by qualified professionals, I find the experience of relaying my innermost feelings to strangers helpful and in many ways cathartic. As I speak, the group rallies around me with words of encouragement and gratitude, and I'm reminded that video games are uniquely placed to help people explore the kind of sensitive and interpersonal issues that can be hard to face up to in real life.

★ ★ ★

I LEARNED A VALUABLE LESSON ABOUT MY UNCLE'S SUICIDE IN *GRAND THEFT AUTO V* ROLE-PLAY

Published by VG24/7 – *Tuesday, November 12, 2019*

I'm standing on the corner of Innocence Boulevard and Crusade Road, east of Strawberry. Before me is the Central Los Santos Medical Center and, atop one of the hospital's front-facing helipads, is a man threatening to jump. In the three or so years I've spent mucking around in *Grand Theft Auto V*'s unofficial player-made role-play servers, this is the first time I've encountered a scenario of this nature.

As I approach the pavement closest to the building's edge, the man tells me I've come close enough. Yelling down, he tells me that if I make for the ladder at the far side of the car park, or if I call the in-game emergency services, another civilian, or post anything on Bleeter – *GTA V*'s slant on Twitter, which doubles as this server's public IM text chat – he'll throw himself from the ledge. I tell the man that I pose no threat, and that I'm simply curious as to why he's got himself so worked up.

'Take it easy, mate,' I say. 'What's your name?'

'Shaun,' he replies. 'I'm just fucking fed up. I don't know what else to do.'

Shaun explains that his late friend, who'd struggled with mental health issues, slipped from a station platform into the path of an oncoming train. He says that while he's unsure of the authorities' findings, the police have since determined his mate's passing as suicide. Shaun says his friend, Steve, was like any other guy in his early 20s – a great laugh, into sports – and had just landed an electrician's apprenticeship with a respected local firm. He was smart, had a lovely girlfriend and, in Shaun's eyes, had everything going for him. Shaun says Steve's parents are expectedly distraught, and his friends are struggling to cope.

In a game otherwise associated with crude, over the top, law-breaking hedonism, the *GTA V* role-play scene offers a nuanced take on the sandbox crime simulator's vanilla state. Its myriad modded servers let players live virtual lives closer to reality, which in turn creates scope for the very real scenario painted by Shaun. That's not to say Shaun himself isn't role-playing a make-believe tale – RP server rules encourage players to craft and commit to credible and meticulous backstories – but the situation he describes appears heartfelt and sincere.

Away from stealing cars, running drugs and offing unscrupulous mobsters, I once happened upon a group of role-players who use San Andreas as a safe space to cope with grief, gambling, and addiction. But this is the first time I've encountered such a personal conversation one-on-one.

I tell Shaun that in 2008 my uncle took his own life, and that my family and I also struggled to balance grief with the inevitable uncertainty and 'what ifs' that followed. Shaun tells me he totally gets that, and recently lost his head with one mate for suggesting Steve had taken the "coward's way out". He says that while he's insightful enough himself to realise his pal is probably still in shock, they all are, this stigma-driven attitude upsets him.

I tell Shaun that I know exactly where he's coming from, and that he's right, everyone deals with things differently and

quite often people say things out of turn that they don't necessarily mean, or, worse, understand. I tell Shaun that my own
bugbear is when people say 'X person didn't seem like the type
that'd kill themselves', because rarely does anyone who follows
through with taking their own life seem so lost or desperate.
Well-intentioned as the sentiment is, it gets my back up. I then
explain to Shaun that I'm certain had my uncle been able to
open up about how he was feeling, he'd still be with us today.
That said, I'm equally sure that there was nothing anyone could
have done beforehand, and that my uncle Jim's passing was no
one's fault – not his own, nor our family's.

I tell Shaun that being able to resolve these distinctly jarring
points in my head took such a long time, and that while I can't
speak for Steve, or anyone else for that matter, I am of the view
this dichotomy is one of the few universal truths of suicide.

A long silence follows, broken momentarily by far-off sirens
and echoing gunshots. It's easy to forget we're having this
conversation within *Grand Theft Auto V*'s Los Santos, a city that
never sleeps.

'I'm going to come up the ladder,' I eventually say. Shaun
stays silent. I hop the hedge that runs the length of the complex,
dart across the car park and climb up the side of the building.

My avatar approaches Shaun's, and I ask if he's okay. He says
yes. At this point, if this were real-life, I reckon we might hug,
shake hands, or at least high five. Instead, my avatar points at
Shaun's. He points back, then raises his hands above his head
in a 'don't shoot'-type pose. I do the same, and then Shaun
drops into a prone position and immediately jumps back to

his feet. The limitations of the server's emote systems brings welcomed levity to what's come before. I laugh. Shaun laughs. And then I about turn, and make my way back down to street-level. Shaun follows, we exchange brief goodbyes, and then set off in opposite directions.

On my way back to Legion Square, the server's de-facto meeting point, I can't help but compare my encounter with Shaun to my own experience with suicide. Again, I can't say for sure if Shaun was for real, but I've no reason to believe he wasn't. Had he decided to jump from atop the Central Los Santos Medical Centre, the only in-game consequence he'd have suffered would have been an eight-minute incapacitation penalty, before respawning at the front door of the very same hospital building.

Still, talking through his story made me realise, or perhaps reaffirm, two things: talking helps and everyone's situation is different. In real life, Shaun has more grieving, processing, and, hopefully, talking and sharing ahead of him as he comes to terms with his loss. Doing so, in reality, is not always straightforward – I once tried and failed to engage with cognitive behavioural therapy – which makes in-game encounters like these all the more powerful.

Shaun and my conversation, albeit in-game, put me in the shoes of the listener – something which I wish so, so much I could have been for my uncle Jim. And yet, it changes nothing. No one is to blame, and Jim wasn't ready or able to open up about his darkest feelings. Ultimately, suicide is such a specific, idiosyncratic thing, even if parallels can be drawn between the victims and their families in the wake of each devastating act.

With all of this said, *Grand Theft Auto V* – a six-year-old video game rooted in violent virtual crime – is hardly the place you'd expect profound and poignant moments like this to occur. When my uncle took his own life over 11 years ago, I sought escapism in video games more than ever before. I've since spent several hundred hours combing this particular crime sim's urban, suburban and rural sprawl, and yet I'm still blown away by touching instances like the one I experienced with Shaun. Again, CBT didn't work for me when my mental health dipped in real life, but these exchanges, inside virtual worlds and within a safe framework, are invaluable – to myself, to Shaun, and to anyone else who has something to share.

CHAPTER 11

THE GREEN T-SHIRT

(OR, THE STORY OF THE TIME I THOUGHT I WAS GOING TO KILL MYSELF)

I've never told anyone this story. Well, actually that's a lie. I once blurted out a rabbled, steaming drunk version of this story to my girlfriend Jenny at four in the morning during a drinking session not long after it happened, before waking up not entirely sure if the conversation had actually taken place. When she raised it with me again on a different rabbled, steaming drunk night out not long after that, I got defensive.

The thing about depression – in my experience, at least – is that suicidal thoughts are never too far from the surface. For me, especially when I'm in the middle of a slump, or if I've had a particularly bad day or week, I become more acutely aware of them. Over the years I have become increasingly better at identifying them, and today I'm able to keep them at arm's length pretty much all the time and am no longer scared of them. I'd

go as far to say I'm in total control of them, and that they just...
exist, somewhere in the background. Which is nice (as nice as
it can be).

This wasn't always the case. But before I get to the green
t-shirt story, I need to explain the green t-shirt itself.

Five months after Jim killed himself, Jenny and I went to Ibiza for
a two week holiday. We hit the clubs, partied hard and did a fair
whack of drinking. By the tenth successive day of debauchery,
we opted to have a relatively chilled one down San Antonio's
West End. We went to Ground Zero, a rock & roll bar at the
bottom of the strip, bought a couple of drinks and grabbed a
quiet-ish corner of the room for a chat. We'd hardly returned
from the bar when a group of four well-oiled lads brushed past,
one of whom licked his thumb and ran it down Jenny's cheek,
blowing her a kiss as he did. Jenny was mortified. I was raging. I
shouted the boy back, but he told me in no uncertain terms to
'get fucked' as he swaggered towards the exit. I saw red, dropped
my pint and made a beeline for the prick, because *who the fuck
did he think he was*? I've never once started a fight in my life, but
have occasionally resorted to violence in defence of friends and
family. I'm not particularly proud of it, but in this instance, Jenny
had been targeted and she agreed I'd reacted in the same way she
would had if the shoe had been on the other foot.

Anyway, I made a run for the face-licker, who now had his
back to me. As he made his way through the doorway of the
main dancefloor towards the stairs, I cracked him on the back
of the head. He turned, aggrieved, and I put him on his arse

with a right-hand haymaker. He folded like a deck of cards. I felt like a cross between Robin Hood and Muhamad Ali, taking a second or two to admire my work... momentarily forgetting I'd pushed this poor bastard's three pals out of the road to get to him, who'd in turn watched the melee unfold from ringside. Crash. Bang. Wallop. I was sent two feet into the air, before crashing to the floor, before then getting my head kicked in by four very drunk and very upset Englishmen. Worse still, Jenny, panicked amid the chaos, had dashed for the door to intervene, and had slipped on the spilled pint I'd discarded moments prior. The club's two on-duty bouncers had rightly responded by seeing if she was okay and getting her back to her feet. Meanwhile, yer auld da was getting a tanking in the hallway outside the toilets. By the time the bouncers finally caught up with the brawl, I was sprawled out on the deck, and the back of my green t-shirt was torn to shreds. I dusted myself off, reunited with Jenny and thought it best we stagger back to the Galeria Hotel to get washed and changed. After midnight, the West End of San Antonio was crawling with messy, hedonistic revellers, spilling from loud and smoky clubs, spewing their rings at the side the of the road. A roughed-up 22 year old man stoating by with a ripped shirt and a fat lip was hardly untoward, but, still, I was embarrassed. I'd lost my cool and had behaved in an outward manner that mirrored and amplified the pent-up blackness I felt inside.

When we arrived back to our hotel, instead of tossing my green t-shirt it in the bin, I bundled it into my suitcase with the rest of my dirty clothes. I'm not sure why.

Before my mum retired, when I was still living with her and my dad, she'd send our ironing to a shop around the corner, which meant each item came back nicely pressed and resting on a hanger. I realise this sounds dead posh but I think it was more a reflection of how little time my mum had in the house and how lazy my dad and I were. My clothes were stationed on the chin-up bar I'd mounted to my doorframe, and, two weeks after returning from the White Isle, there was my battle-scarred green t-shirt among them – in tatters, but washed, dried and ironed all the same. Back from Ibiza, five months after Jim's death, with no other distractions on the horizon, my undiagnosed depression was at its worst. I was as low as I'd ever been in my life, and had started having real, tangible suicidal thoughts. I cringed at the sight of the green t-shirt, because it represented behaviour I was ashamed of, the emotions that turned my stomach and, whether I realised it or not, the blackness that hung over me. I felt the distinct urge to wrap the green t-shirt around my neck. I did, very briefly, tightening and loosening, letting my imagination run ahead of me. I did this for about ten minutes, tightening a little more, holding it a half second or so longer each time. I became so consumed in what I was doing, to the point where it felt like I'd lost control. It was surreal and devastating and exhilarating all at once. At that moment, my dad came home from work and slammed the door on his way in. He shouted hello from downstairs. I dropped the t-shirt, shouted back, and scuttled into my room. I closed my bedroom door and burst into tears.

I cried for about an hour, mostly because I felt like shit and didn't really understand why; and partly because I'd become gravely aware of what I was doing before. I started second-guessing what might have been and what might have happened had my dad not arrived home when he did. I was terrified. I sat in silence with my hands under my chin at the bottom of my bed until I felt like moving. I stared up at the room's sloping roof and chord of the green metal IKEA lampshade that I'd had since I was at school. It got dark outside.

Later that night, my colleagues had arranged an online game of *GTA IV*. I was still a plumber at the time so jumped into a game with my former tradesman and two of the firm's younger apprentices – one of whom had just started with the company. We played without headsets and communicated with individual texts to one another, about missions, the best in-game guns, and how terrible we all were at this game compared to everyone else online. At one point, while piling into the same car, my old boss teased the new guy by revving the vehicle forward ever so slightly every time he tried to open the back door. It was a dose of Marx Brothers, Laurel and Hardy, Three Stooges-esque slapstick comedy that I absolutely needed, it sent me rolling with laughter around the floor, texting each one of my peers madly about how funny the set-piece was – and this was why playing online was the future of video games.

I've never told anyone that story until now. Not really. Not properly. I thought about putting it at the beginning of *Checkpoint*, and then decided against it. It is unquestionably a huge part of my mental health journey, and it feels nice to finally share it, but it by no means defines it. Everything else you've read to this point has been equally important to me, and probably has more scope to speak to others. That said, if there ever was an example of the power of video games as a means of escapism, for me, the aftermath of the green t-shirt story is it.

For over ten years now, I've lived with depression and anxiety and I consider that evening as one of the lowest points of my life. Was I ever going to follow through? In hindsight, I don't think so. At the time I was convinced that I was. The fact that I can't be sure terrifies me even now. I also consider that about of *GTA IV* silliness among mates one of the most important gaming sessions of my life. That evening, I wasn't in the right frame of mind to be around people, despite how much I might have needed it. And yet *Grand Theft Auto IV*, a game synonymous with murder and death, saved my mood and, potentially, my life by allowing me to connect with my friends remotely in a less formal space. Liberty City, the game's digital incarnation and pseudo slant on New York City will forever hold a special place in my heart.

A NEW CHALLENGER APPEARS

LUNA MARTINEZ

Luna is a video games and music writer whose 2019 article 'How Bloodborne *helped me transition gender and choose a new name' explores how she used the character creation suite in From Software's action role-playing game* Bloodborne *as a means of expression that eventually helped her transition. Despite the myriad of outlandish and iterative options often offered by character creators, she always strives to craft characters that (somewhat) resemble her in real life. For Luna, doing so in* Bloodborne *allowed her to craft a character that resembled how she saw herself in real life, before making changes beyond the game itself.*

'I think of gender as puzzle, which is an analogy that can help people better understand the process. While cisgender people may not understand having issues with their own gender, everyone has issues with understanding themselves. We're all figuring ourselves out so framing it like that helps.

'I grew up in the closet and when I was young I didn't even have the words to express that I was trans. Not knowing how to even describe what I felt was difficult. For me, video games are my biggest hobby along with music. Video games aren't only escapism for me, but the ability to play from different perspectives helps me grow as a person. Also, as mentioned in the article, being able to play as myself helps me. I think video games are as important as any art in terms of mental health; as all art should be an outlet to let us deal with our feelings.

'Video games are also where I first played around with gender, even if it was as simple as just playing as a girl character. Being able to experiment with my gender in a safe space was a big deal. In terms of video games' power to convey information and tell stories, I don't think their interactive nature makes them necessarily more important than other mediums, but the strengths are different. What makes them interesting is the way it can help us see things from other perspectives. If I play *Assassin's Creed* I feel like an assassin, whereas watching a movie would feel like watching someone else. This is important as it can help bridge the divide between minorities. It's why I think representation is important – partly for people like me to be able to see ourselves, but also so people can understand us on a human level.

'Video games have the power to bridge divides in ways other media can't. The lack of diversity in gaming is a tragedy because I truly believe it would be a great first step to bridging our divides. It's ignorant to suggest video games would solve all our issues, but even small victories are victories and worth fighting for.

'For trans players, I think having the option to both change character names and their appearance is important. At least for me, I'm usually very happy with the character I make at the beginning and use it as escapism. However, the ability to change appearance at any time is true to my real life experience. I see no reason to not have both unless the main character is a defined character.

'In *Bloodborne*, I viewed the character I'd created as an extension of my real self. It was incredibly empowering. It happened at the same time I was dealing with coming out. *Bloodborne* is also an incredible game which helped. There really aren't words I can use to describe the feeling of being able to see myself and take control of my destiny so to speak.

'In an action-oriented game like *Bloodborne,* the game's characters are secondary to their worlds and non-playable characters. I think, overall, video games owe trans people more in the way of representation. Even if I didn't think of games being important, I think it's important for people like me to see ourselves. Maybe I would have come out years ago if I'd seen a trans character and knew it was normal and okay. We owe people to represent the diversity of the human experience. How many gay or black, or any minority people would still be alive if they got to see themselves and know they aren't playing second-fiddle to straight white men. Everyone deserves to play video games and be happy.'

CHAPTER 12

BEING SAFE IN OUR WORLD

CHARITIES & SUPPORT

❝ I had someone close to me that tried to kill himself.' Leo Zullo, Managing Director of independent video game publishing company Wired Productions, is very honest during our interview. 'I had to literally pick him up and take him to the hospital. It was a bit hard to deal with and it was very real.'

Later that same year, Zullo's uncle took his own life. A few months after that, his friend was sectioned under the UK's Mental Health Act, in what he describes as a brutal year. In late 2019, Zullo founded the video games and mental health charity Safe In Our World, alongside his colleagues and friends Neil Broadhead and Gareth Williams, to foster positive mental health and wellbeing in and around video games, for both players and developers. The renowned mental health axiom 'it's okay to not be okay' sits at the forefront of the charity's operations, which is run and represented by several trustees, ambassadors and patrons – all voluntarily.

The idea was born from the heartbreaking run of events he faced, combined with an overriding desire to eliminate the stigmas and stereotypes tied to mental health discussions. The charity targets those with personal experience of mental illness, directly or indirectly, and those without – helping the latter group better understand mental illness, and to become more adept in identifying symptoms and signs. Another driving factor to these charitable ambitions was his time spent promoting LKA's *Town of Light*, and, being of Italian descent himself, his empathy for the one-time patrons of the now shuttered Volterra mental health institution.

'My cousin has paranoid schizophrenia – he's one of the five per cent that can't be treated,' Zullo explains. 'When we were helping LKA promote the console versions of *The Town of Light*, I met with the doctors and Luca of LKA himself. I visited Volterra and was shocked to learn how the patients were once treated there, and the general atrocities tied to mental health and mental illness in those days in general. Had they not shut the Volterra down, my cousin would have been a patient at that very institution.

'Fast forward a few years, in the early days of planning Safe In Our World, we decided to donate money to the US mental health and video games charity Take This. Giving money, it definitely helps, but it's a very isolated thing to do. We wanted to do more. Mental illness was this thing throughout all our lives – the sequence of events that happened to my friends and my uncle made us think about how we could really help people in our industry. There needed to be some substance to what we're doing. We wanted to have a bit of impact, to genuinely help people, and not just focus on raising awareness. Don't get me wrong, raising awareness is crucial, but we also wanted to add some meat to the bones of what we were doing.'

SafeInOurWorld.org boasts a news section that's curated with important, relevant and contemporary mental health and video games-related stories; it highlights games that the charity believes to be worth showcasing and so-called 'hero stories' that detail specific tales from charity team members, those within the games industry and beyond. They are also working on a set of policies pertaining to mental health in the workplace, which ask companies to help their employees – if they can persuade employers within the games industry to treat mental health as a key concern within their organisations, that ethos can improve the working environment itself.

While Zullo notes that they'd love companies to engage fully with their policies, one of Safe in Our World's overarching goals is to educate employers and employees so that they're better able to help those struggling with mental health issues on an advisory level.

Although it was a volunteer-driven organisation at the time of discussion, Safe In Our World has their sights set on being fully operational by the end of the year with a number of full-time staff members as it garners more official support from the games industry across the globe. They aim to raise income to do so via mental health-focused games such as Emily Mitchell's

BAFTA award-winning *Fractured Minds*; just 16 years old when winning, she is now a core member of the charity's team, and the game – Zullo feels – typifies their outlook perfectly.

'One thing we can't do, at this stage at least, is offer medical care, so we need to act a conduit between the video games world and the medical world. We also want to share as many positive stories as we can from within, people putting themselves out there, putting themselves on the line, and in turn, allowing people to relate to other people telling their very personal experiences. Everyone's own story is different, it's personal, it's unique, but at the same time there are often similarities and overlapping aspects.

'Safe in Our World will lobby the United Kingdom's government to achieve a true understanding of the power of video games to serve as a positive medium in assisting people with mental health issues. Likewise, the charity will challenge the government to jump-start and promote a national conversation, to create a better support infrastructure for those who suffer from mental illness. We also intend to reach out to other governments whenever possible to promote these policies and drive conversations about mental health awareness around the world.'

* * *

When I first speak to Dr Sachin Shah over Skype, he tells me that I've picked the perfect day to do so. Had we spoken 24 hours prior, he'd have been forced to tell me that Gaming The Mind was a collective of mental health professionals and psychiatrists who have particular interests in video games. But, having been granted official charity status on the morning of our call, he can instead tell me: they are now officially a video game charity.

Regardless of status, their promotion of positive mental health within the gaming community and industry is invaluable. With a distinct focus on the intersection between video games and mental health, their remit is to raise awareness while reducing misinformed stigma in the process. Gaming The Mind doesn't pathologise, instead it questions the nature of mental health stereotypes in popular culture, challenges games with unreliable narrators, considers games that test identity stereotypes and explores video games that put you in the shoes of someone with issues of mental health.

Through their mission, Gaming The Mind has positioned itself as a hugely reliable and relatable resource on social media – particularly on Twitter. Dr Shah himself runs the account, which endeavours to share positive games and stories, worthwhile schemes and programmes, and video games which go that extra mile to tackle the often sensitive and interpersonal themes associated with mental illness.

'My favourite thing about Twitter is when people reply to our stuff and comment saying *this game really moved me*, or *this game really gave me different take on what I'm going through.* What I enjoy pushing is when someone online writes an account of how games helped them get through a tough time or helped them understand what they're experiencing. If I can help promote, then there's a chance that other people can pick it up and relate to further. Sometimes the things we share in turn get shared out by clinicians, so we are slowly filtering through this narrative that games have a very valid thing to say about mental health.

'I'm also keen to keep a balance, though. We're not here to be cheerleaders for the industry and medium entirely. We will call out games when they're not good, with representation or whatever it may be.

'We want to be balanced, and there's a trap that can be fallen into where you're so dedicated to showing games as positive, where you end up over-arguing in their favour. For example, I have no reason to believe that video games can cure depression. I've not seen any such evidence. But I have seen stories who find games therapeutic in a different kind of way – as stress relievers, or as escapism, or as something that builds their resilience and shows them that they can power through. Games like *Celeste* or *Sekiro* or *Dark Souls*. With these games, the player is taught that if they keep trying then they can carry on, and I think it's possible to translate that ethos to real life.'

Translating that ethos to real life is made possible by the fact each member of Gaming The Mind is a video game hobbyist in their own time. Before establishing the charity, its members worked in the South London and Maudsley Trust, a mental health foundation comprised of psychiatric trainees. It was there that an organisation named Reading The Mind explored mental health in literature; Gaming The Mind riffs directly off of that. What started as regular but casual meet ups, grew to brainstorming sessions, charitable activities and monthly debates. With their professional expertise and leisure interests, the group felt they were uniquely placed to offer insights into games and mental health.

'Some of what I'm most proud of are our efforts around mental health education in the gaming community,' adds Dr Shah. 'Podcasts, blogs, social media presence – when you do that through the lens of video games, you're speaking the same language as people. So, you get through to a different crowd that the NHS can get through to.'

These avenues help reach a broader range of people, whether that's younger people who don't engage as much with national bodies, or reaching a greater male audience, who can be difficult to reach with general mental health messaging. They've also done great work within the mental health profession itself, deconstructing the idea that games are something to be afraid of. They've held talks and conferences to show what games are about, what they cover, what issues they should be worried about, at the same time raising points there's still not enough information on. This has escalated to parliament – advising on legislation, white papers, and contributing to inquiries around gaming addiction and more.

As the world continues to change, it's reassuring to know that there are people like Gaming The Mind advocating at all levels. While they do so, gaming continues to flourish, particularly around topics of mental health, and it shows no sign of slowing.

'Not every game has to be *League of Legends* or *Warcraft*,' Dr Shah assures. 'Some can speak more narratively and have deeper meanings.'

★ ★ ★

In 2012, Matt Hughes – a talented freelance journalist – took his own life. Unbeknownst to the editors, he'd built sound working relationships with through of his impressive writing, Hughes had suffered from depression and shortly before his passing he sent an email around his employers informing them he'd no longer be available for work.

Two of those editors, Russ Pitts and Susan Arendt, realised that while they had working relationships with dozens of industry peers, the majority of their conversations with those people took place online, in text and not in person. Shortly after this, Pitts and Arendt founded video games charity Take This, with a mission statement to inform our community about mental health issues, to provide education about mental disorders and mental illness prevention, and to help reduce the stigma of mental illness.

Today, Take This provides comprehensive resources, support and consultation from a member of mental health staff and medical professionals, all of which is tailored for the needs of game developers and players alike. They strive to embrace the diverse cultures of the video games community, in a safe, open and understanding environment; one of its main focuses is crunch – the process where video game developers are forced to work long, unreasonable hours to finish specific parts of video games ahead of their release.

'Mental health needs to be part of the conversation, and it needs to be a conversation that's had in a healthy way,' says Eve Crevoshay, Executive Director of Take This. 'We explore what it's like to work in games, finding out what are the mental health impacts of being a game industry employee. Those can be really tough. At our heart, we were founded as an organisation to champion and be the voice of people who make games. We're also the voice of people who play games and care about mental health, and, increasingly, we want to provide information and advice backed-up by scientific research whenever and wherever we can.'

They've recently hired a researcher to focus on game-informed data on topics including hate speech, recruitment and propaganda in games and game-adjacent spaces online, and have released two white papers on the industry itself – the first on crunch's negative impact on game developers' mental health.

'How do we use the research and knowledge that's out there to help people that make games have better work experiences and healthier careers over time? Our primary areas of concern are, overall, burnout, stress and something we call "allostatic load" – which is the combined physical, emotional and mental effects of uncertainty and job stress, studio closures, and crunch. We also talk about inclusion and diversity and how the mental health of people who are not a majority is particularly affected in the game industry. It's such a white male dominated work force, and we touch upon how that impacts the way choices are made about what games show up, and what games are made and what they look like when they're done.'

One of Take This' primary areas of focus is the public perception of those who make video games. The industry lives so much of its existence on platforms such as Twitter, so they consider the potential negative impact social media has on game developers and players' mental health. Take This is also concerned with 'games as naked evil', as Crevoshay put it, where video games are demonised in the public eye. Video games are a lot of things to a lot of people, and there is therefore a diverse range of ways they are engaged with. Moral panic derails the diversity of that and the host of wonderful things video games can do and actually be for people.

One of Take This' flagship initiatives are its AFK (Away From Keyboard) rooms at North American gaming conventions, where attendees can seek quiet spaces away from the hustle and bustle of the show floors, all of which are staffed by clinical and non-clinical volunteers. These rooms also serve as a way for people to start the conversation about their mental health challenges. Their role is to be as consistently present and available at as many events and places as possible, normalising mental health struggles as something not to be ashamed of talking about.

'Can perception be changed?' asks Crevoshay. 'I think, actually, yes. It's a "yes... but". The game industry has changed quite significantly in the last ten years. There is a lot less crunch than their used to be, and that's great news. That said, there is a real dichotomy in the industry around who thinks crunch is good and who thinks crunch is bad. There is a subset of the industry that continues to perceive crunch as a necessary aspect of the process of making games, and will not let go of that. That's most visible in the cases of highly successful games that are achieved through crunch, such as

Grand Theft Auto. Rockstar is infamous for crunch, and they have really successful games. Everybody is willing to say, *well, the best games that are made right now are made as a result of crunch. Therefore, we need crunch to make good games.*

'That's a really sad state of affairs because the research, if you go back and look at Metacritic scores and reports of crunch, high rates of crunch in fact correlate with lower scores overall. It's really simple. That shift is just going to take time, unfortunately.

'There are some persistent myths about making games that shift harder. The most pernicious is that we make games because we're passionate about them – if we're passionate about games then it shouldn't matter how much we work and how much crunch we have. It doesn't matter that we get burnt out because "we're passionate about games and that solves everything". The idea that passion has to equal crunch or this over the top display of loyalty – that is a false equivalency.'

Take This is full of people who will never tire of helping the world at large understand that the stigma of mental health is a real thing. Crevoshay's advice to anyone suffering in silence is simple: speak to someone.

'There are lots of people out there who are talking about their mental health, and that's really exciting,' she continues. 'It takes a lot of bravery to talk about it but you only need to talk about it with one person and it will make you feel so much better. So many times, when I say that I work in a mental health organisation, I watch people open up physically, they relax, they know they can talk about it with me, they're relieved. We want to highlight the representation of mental health and mental illness in games, to make it normalised there, so that the conversation just keeps going everywhere.

'Yes, it is hard, but you don't have to tell everybody. It's okay just to tell one person, and that will start the conversation and help you get to a place where you can get the help that you need.'

* * *

There are so many organisations doing remarkable work, and there is not enough time to spotlight all of them. But here's a start:

The AbleGamers Foundation – ablegamers.org
Also known as the AbleGamers Charity, it is a non-profit public charity that aims to improve the overall quality of life for those with disabilities through the power of video games.

Child's Play – childsplaycharity.org
Child's Play improves the lives of children in hospitals and other child facilities through the power of play.

CheckPoint – checkpointorg.com
CheckPoint is a charity that provides mental health resources for gamers and the gaming community. (Not affiliated with this book!)

Desert Bus For Hope – desertbus.org
Desert Bus for Hope combines video games and tedium to benefit charity and is the world's longest running internet-based fundraiser.

Extra Life – extra-life.org
Extra Life unites thousands of gamers around the world to play games in support of their local Children's Miracle Network Hospital.

Games Done Quick – gamesdonequick.com
Games Done Quick is a series of charity video game marathons. These events feature high-level gameplay by speedrunners raising money for charity.

Gaming The Mind – gamingthemind.org
Doctors by day; gamers by night! Exploring interactions between mental health/gaming and promoting wellbeing in the gaming community.

Humble Bundle – humblebundle.com
Humble Bundle sells games and other digital content – their mission is to support charity while providing awesome content.

Safe In Our World – safeinourworld.org
As a mental health charity, their mission is to foster positive mental health wellbeing & deliver support for gamers and the UK games industry.

Special Effect – specialeffect.org.uk

The UK-based charity that's levelling the playing field for gamers with physical disabilities.

Take This – takethis.org

Take This was founded to let people know that there's help for people with mental health challenges who are also passionate about making games.

CHAPTER 13

FOR THE PLAYERS

BROADCAST 4 REPS & SUPPORT

It's easy to escape reality in online worlds. *EVE Online* is one of the greatest in scope – launched in 2003 and set 21,000 years into the future, it swaps sage and sorcery for sci-fi and space-crafts. Similar to the *Grand Theft Auto V* role-play community, *EVE*'s half a million players work as space-age manufacturers; traders, pirates, scammers, con artists, honest Johns, miners, and a wealth of other trades, across its 7,800+ star systems – each one of which is accessible to players.

If any of that sounds intimidating, that's because it is. You're not alone – I've tried and failed to get into *EVE* over the years because breaking its complex veneer requires time, loads and loads – and loads – of time, and there were always so many games that need playing each week, month and year. I envy those who have mastered traversing these vast worlds. So, it's little surprise those who do commit to *EVE* do so wholeheartedly.

Despite its in-universe scandals, murders, high profile heists, mass graveyards, hostile propaganda – all generated by inspired and conniving players from the comfort of their homes – *EVE* is a welcoming and connected community; in fact, it's probably one of the most welcoming in the video game industry. Sure, most of its veterans will stab you in the back as quickly as they'll offer salutations, but it's all in the name of the game.

So when struggles extend beyond the game and back to the reality many have been escaping, the *EVE* community is both ready and equipped to listen. Broadcast 4 Reps is *EVE*'s in-game mental health initiative, launched in 2015 following the passing of long-serving player John Bellicose, who sadly took his own life. Spearheaded by fellow *EVE* player Coffee Rocks of the Brave Newbies faction, the launch was marked by a YouTube video showing clips from players, employees from the game's developer CCP, and John's mother – known as 'Mom Bellicose' – all appealing to those struggling with poor mental health to speak out and not suffer in silence. With the motto 'You'll Never Fly Alone' front and centre, their mission is clear.

Broadcast 4 Reps has its own in-game chat channel within *EVE*, its own Discord channel outside of the game, and is staffed by volunteers who make themselves available to chat, publicly or privately, as required. Lukas 'Jezaja' Hielscher and Glenn 'Tovanis' Patterson are two volunteers who have been playing *EVE* for ten years, and got involved with the initiative shortly after launch. Stationed on either side of the Atlantic – Tovanis in the States, Jezaja in Germany – both players look after Broadcast 4 Reps across time-zones.

Though the pair didn't know John Bellicose personally, the story of his passing moved many within the game, themselves included, and they wanted to help others in need. Jezaja had seen first-hand numerous cases of young people taking their own lives through his former work at a funeral home, and wanted to actively help prevent further loss of life where he could through Broadcast 4 Reps.

This can be as simple as monitoring their in-game channel and Discord server; there are ebbs and flows across the year – with peaks around holiday seasons – but when someone reaches out, whether just looking for an ear to listen or something more serious, they are there.

'The *EVE* community is older than other game communities,' notes Jezaja. '*EVE* players, on average, are somewhere between 30 and 50 years old, and this is also the main age of young men who kill themselves. Awareness of this is one of the main reasons why I wanted to join.

'We are not professionals. We're simply trying to provide the missing link between the player who seeks help and the potential professional who they might seek out afterwards. Being part of Broadcast 4 Reps can be challenging, but I see it like any other community now.

'I personally separate how I play in *EVE*. I'm in the low sec and sometimes I play the game like an asshole. I might be killing newbies, I might wait in cloak ships to pounce on people – this sort of stuff is the norm for most *EVE* players. If people approach me I can quickly switch to being diplomatic.'

Tovanis feels the same; he splits his time between regular

nightshift employment, playing *EVE* for fun, hosting Broadcast 4 Reps and running his faction's video output on Twitch. So committed is he to his *EVE* endeavours that he has a six-monitor set-up at home, with half-a-dozen 32" screens all focused on different things.

'I have Discord on one screen that's in eye-shot,' he explains. 'That means that if I spot something happening, I can immediately attend to it. Once that's taken care of, I can immediately go back to what I was doing. If I have to multitask, that's what I do.'

The dedication of Broadcast 4 Reps' volunteers is astounding, so willing and able to drop everything to offer an ear to someone in need. It is a simple thing, but in the right circumstance: it can be everything. For me, *Grand Theft Auto V* is my most-played game online; while I've uncovered a handful of powerful mental health-related stories within its own alternative reality, I did so by chance. It makes me consider the potential for support systems like this being more broadly integrated into games.

'I think, in theory, it could work in other games. Four or so years ago, there was a similar player community established in *League of Legends*, but it was only active for 12 months. It's not all about being this organised, or big community that's dedicated to mental health and mental health awareness – it's about listening to your mates who may be suffering. You can do this in any game. If you're in a *World of Warcraft* guild, and your favourite Dwarf Rogue is in a bad mood, or they don't want to contribute any more – you can just ask how they're doing. *Hey, what's going on, why are you not happy about this new quest? This new item? This new mission?* It's about relationships, in guilds, in player communities, where you can have an open ear to just simply ask people to talk to you. Sometimes it can be as straightforward as that.'

What is less straightforward is the toll on being an active participant in Broadcast 4 Reps can have on its members. The naysayers are a vocal minority, but still, even considering the good Broadcast 4 Reps does and the great service it provides within *EVE*, working round the clock, listening to other people's problems, and offering advice isn't easy. Even writing this book, revisiting some of the darkest moments in my life, it has exhausted me, and the thought of being there for someone else – people you're more often than not meeting for the first time – at a moment's notice is an admirable but truly daunting prospect indeed.

'Sometimes when people are really down... pulling them back up and onto their feet isn't easy, but that's the nature of how it works and the responsibility we accept and expect from ourselves,' acknowledges Tovanis. 'In a perfect world we wouldn't need Broadcast 4 Reps at all. However, knowing how things are in general as far as mental health is concerned – I'm going to keep doing whatever I can do to help people.'

Striking a balance between real life, their leisure time, their leisure time inside *EVE* and their time represented as Broadcast 4 Reps is – while difficult at times – crucial. Yet, the feeling of being able to impact people's lives and support them makes the hardships worth it. The feedback sticks with them too – not to inflate their egos or prop them up in any way, but simply to show that they are making a difference, no matter how big or small.

'To use the title of your book as an example,' Jezaja posits, 'Broadcast 4 Reps is like a checkpoint for *EVE* players. I hope that Broadcast 4 Reps will last for a long time. But, on the other hand, I also hope that one day we don't need an organisation like ours at all.'

* * *

Esports are an anomaly. Instead of games being an outlet for fun and escape away from the responsibilities of day-to-day life, here they can be someone's career. Professional players get paid big money to compete in tournaments watched by millions worldwide. They train and compete with the same rigorous precision as athletes, battle for prize-pools totalling millions of dollars. They commit endless hours every day to their craft: this is video gaming at the highest level.

Take a look at other sports – football, tennis or swimming, for example. A peak athlete is surrounded by opportunity, through wages, accolades, sponsorship and more. They're also surrounded by a team of people, to train them, protect them and ensure their wellbeing in a whirlwind world. It's easy to see esports as far removed from those worlds, so it's a fair question: how does esports, as an industry, compare?

It has, like many sports, become a billion-dollar industry. The industry has grown considerably from only nine esports competitions in 1998, to the over 3000 officially recognised in 2018,[1] an increase of almost 38,000 per cent. Kyle 'Bugha' Giersdorf, a 16-year-old from the USA, claimed top spot from a field of 40 million players at 2019's *Fortnite* World Cup, netting $3m (£2.4m), as one example.[2] The *Call of Duty* World League Pro League boasted a prize purse of $2 million,[3] the *Hearthstone* World Championship – a digital card game – boasted a $1m top tier in 2019.[4] Where the concluding tournament of the *Dota* Pro Circuit – The International 2019 – saw the event's total prize haul jump to a staggering $34.3m.[5]

If those prize pools do not underscore the popularity of esports today, viewing figures do. *Fortnite: Battle Royale* has over 250 million players. Over 1 billion people – 30 per cent of internet users – watch live streams, such as live events, tournaments and 'lets plays'.[6] The UEFA Champions League final was watched by 11.3 million people in the UK in 2019; it's estimated 70 million people will watch an esports final in 2020.[7] The most popular South Korean *League of Legends* player, a chap who goes by the in-game pseudonym 'Faker', has a larger Twitter following than the country's biggest football star, Tottenham Hotspur's Son Heung-min.

Within the gaming world, there are also parallels in pay disparity to on-field counterparts: Tyler 'Ninja' Blevins, the most popular *Fortnite* player in the world, is said to earn around $500,000 (£388,000) per month;[8] whereas the world's highest earning female esports player Sasha 'Scarlett' Hostyn has made $357,338 (£269,000) from playing Blizzard Entertainment's *StarCraft 2* throughout her professional career.[9] The latter earnings aren't to be sniffed at, but considering not one woman featured the top 100

richest esports players list for 2019,[10] representation and renumer-
ation problems extend to the digital realm too. Against Scarlett's
$357k haul, *Dota 2* player Johan 'N0tail' Sundstein topped the
chart with annual earnings of $6,890,592 (£5.34 million); while
Counter Strike: Global Offensive's Finn 'karrigan' Andersen finished
100th, having accrued $849,472 (£659,000).[11]

When Giorgio 'Pow3r' Calandrelli spoke to Men's Health in
2019, he told of how pro esports players adhere to strict training
plans masterminded by in-house coaches, sports psychologists
and nutritionists to maximise their chances of success.[12] Despite
being less physical than more conventional sports, he noted
esports players exercise regularly and maintain a strict balanced
diet to keep their minds sharp and stress levels as low as possible.
He also strongly refuted the idea that playing video games for a
living is easy – the desire to be picked up by the biggest teams,
earn a full-time salary and maintain high performance levels
takes its toll both physically and mentally. 'The stress we are
under every day is massive,' he told Men's Health. 'I've heard of
a lot of people experiencing burnout.'

Anecdotally, then, esports aligns in many ways with its
more conventional counterpart, but games aren't just used
for competition: they can be part of the process to strengthen
their cognitive output. Even on a casual basis, games such as Dr
Kawashima's Brain Training challenges players with mini-games
design to improve their mental processes, perceptual and spatial
skills. Esports players' brains are required to process on-screen
information quicker than casual players and must hone light-
ning-quick reactions and razor-sharp awareness as they comb

sprawling virtual worlds and make multiple decisions at once.[13] In training, players can spend upwards of 12 hours per day in front of their screens, making as many as 400 movements on their mouse and keyboards per minute – four times the average player – which can lead to elevated hearts rates. Esports players can then produce the same amount of cortisol (a hormone related to stress) as race car drivers, and their heart rates can hit 180 beats per minute, the equivalent to that of a marathon runner or an F1 driver.[14]

It's unsurprising, then, to hear of burnout being so prevalent an issue, and that people are working to ensure that wellbeing is a core consideration right up at the highest level of gaming. Dr Atheeshaan Arumuham – who specialises in psychiatry, and works with Gaming the Mind – has addressed burnout and continuous stress in players; by using feedback from esports athletes themselves, he has established guidelines designed to improve player wellness and performance.[15] His eight-step advice schedule includes a recommended eight to nine hours of sleep per night because rapid eye movement (REM) sleep is important for learning, memory and emotional health. Players are encouraged to have at least half an hour of exercise per day to reduce cortisol and tension, and to take continuous breaks during long spells of training. 'Having to process a lot of information at a time can become hard work for the brain,' reads Dr Arumuham's advice. 'Taking time to disconnect and engage in some relaxation techniques can provide the necessary downtime to optimise performance.' Here is where we see how games come full circle: for many they are that place to disconnect from reality, and at a professional level, they are what people need to disconnect from.

Dr Arumuham's recommendations continue to align strongly with that of the world's best known pro-athletes, and – more broadly speaking – those looking to maintain a healthy lifestyle. Eating a balanced diet and being mindful of caffeine consumption is advised – while caffeine can seem like an attractive choice to stay alert, says Dr Arumuham, it can have a detrimental effect on focus over long periods. Energy drinks, for example, are high in caffeine and sugar therefore it's not uncommon for players to experience a sugar crash, where the body reacts to a big intake of sugar by rapidly reducing its blood sugar levels. Fruit and grain bars are preferable sources of energy, as is a balanced diet comprised of five portions of fruit and vegetables per day. Likewise, consuming six to eight glasses of fluid each day – with water or low calorie and low sugar drinks considered best – helps avoid dehydration; and food and drink should only be consumed away from players' computers, in order to help players to disengage and relax.

What's core to his advice is that idea of relaxation. He points players towards NHS-approved apps – such as Chill Panda and Cove, both free – which promote mental wellbeing by incorporating breathing techniques, short exercises, and relaxing sounds.

These acts of self care are a vital part of a bigger picture. *League of Legends* teams ROCCAT and Astralis, for example, have recruited on-staff psychologists to monitor player behaviour and psychological wellbeing; these qualified professionals have helped players identify the areas they need to take pause, resulting in greater self-confidence and team cohesion.

It's but one example of how mental health forms a backbone to their success, both in-game and in reality.

Esports flips the notion of taking a step back from work and responsibility by diving into video games on its head, but they share a common root: mental wellbeing is vital, and there are support systems available, whether it's a full team of psychologists, or someone doing the research to tell you – scientifically and absolutely – to take a step back from the screen, grab a glass of water, and take in some fresh air.

★ ★ ★

Back in *EVE Online*, Jezaja keeps a screenshot of an email he received from a random *EVE* player shortly after helping them. He keeps the conversation as a reminder of the great work Broadcast 4 Reps daily. With the sender's name blacked out Jezaja shared the email with me which spoke of this person reconciling with their parents, finding a girlfriend and getting a new job among other life reaffirming outcomes, all of which the sender attributed to Broadcast 4 Reps and their counselling.

It's easy to get consumed in the bigger picture, when games are being discussed at the highest levels of government, making billions upon billions of dollars, and dividing opinion all over, but it's these small things I like to remember: that games offer these little glimmers of hope, and that they can change someone's life for the better.

A NEW CHALLENGER APPEARS

NICKY CASE

Nicky Case is a Canadian indie developer whose games challenge us to think differently. The first is a semi-autobiographical text-based adventure that asks players to weigh up the pros and cons of coming out to traditionalist, conservative parents. Parables of the Polygons *is a browser game that explores collective cultural bias and how seemingly harmless day-to-day choices can actually result in harmful consequences for segregated communities.*

Case's latest game, Adventures With Anxiety, *offers a unique take on anxiety by placing players in control of anxiety itself, in a bid to make us understand why anxiety exists and function it actually provides.*

'Given where we are now, I don't think *Coming Out Sim* or *Parables of the Polygons* worked – I don't think we got the message spread enough. But seriously, the big thing I've been trying to do more recently is provide more information and potential advice for players. Both *Coming Out Simulator* and *Parables of the Polygons* had a message, but *Adventures With Anxiety* had more specific concrete tips with links to more specific mental health resources.

'*Parables of the Polygons*, for example, the overarching message is that making small changes can change the world – but it doesn't extend beyond the message or offer anything that's properly translatable to real life. *Coming Out Simulator* likewise says: *Hey, you're not alone in this.* But it doesn't give any advice. That's not what the game was supposed to be about, to be fair, but what I've tried to do more of recently is make my games more concretely helpful.

'In *Adventures With Anxiety* you play as anxiety itself. The reason I wanted to design the game like this was because every other game has you play as a human with mental illness. I wanted to have a fresh take on it. I thought to himself: *How do I do that?* I decided that, yes, you could play as the mental disorder itself. I'm glad I made that choice because suddenly the game had the mental health payoff at the points where you have to protect your human in the third chapter – and towards the end when you get to play both sides of the conversation – then it gets into the thick of the game. At this point the game helps you understand what the function of anxiety actually is. It makes you ask: *What is the purpose and function of fear?* It helps answer that by having you play from fear's perspective. The game gets you to empathise with your fear a little bit.

'Playing as anxiety in *Adventures With Anxiety* started as a little bit of a gimmick to make it stand out against other mental health games, but as I started developing the game further, I found that doing so had a real, wholesome purpose. I'm a glad that happened.

'From the very beginning I wanted it to be a narrative-style fighting game. No matter which choices you selected the health bar would drop the same amount, but in the early version of the game, you had to try to find out what the human's anxieties were, and you could have your attacks miss. After I while, I decided that this method meant the game became too much of a frustrating experience. It was more distancing as well, because the player was expected to try and outsmart the human, and at that point, you could no longer put yourself in the human's shoes.

'I then completely dropped the more mechanical side of the fighting game and had it as a bit of a light metaphor on top of all of it. The player could put themselves in the shoes of both the anxiety and the human's shoes at the same time – instead of it almost becoming this weird puzzle game.

'I did a lot of research. I spent a lot of time searching through Google Scholar, trying to find out what the most cutting-edge research says about specific areas of mental health, specifically anxiety and psychotherapy. The most interesting and frustrating find was the Dodo Bird Verdict. It's a bit controversial, but the verdict essentially says that after trying and comparing different types of therapies to treat anxiety – be that CBT, psychodynamic, humanist, whatever – all therapies, might be, equally as good at treating the problem. After all of this time! The name of the verdict comes from a *Through the Looking Glass, Alice in Wonderland* quote which says:"All are winners, and thus all must have prizes." What's it's essentially suggesting is that all psycho-therapies do have an impact, but perhaps don't statistically do better than each other. The differences are so small that 30 years later, we're still debating it.

'The best feedback I've had from players is from the ones who've told me the game was recommended to them by their therapist. To think that my game is actually being used in a therapy centre is really heartening. Likewise, it's pretty reassuring to know that, yes, this game which I've worked hard on does have therapeutic value. I like the fact that the game has helped people see their fears as something which has a function, not just some glitch in their heads. To put it crudely – fear doesn't always do its job properly, and that's where anxiety stems from. There can be false positives. It's a guard dog. It's an alarm, and all alarms have false positives.

'To hold a mirror up to how depressing and anxiety-provoking social media can be… that was my plan and it also stems from personal experience. One big motivation for me in making *Adventures With Anxiety* was that I made it for myself. I had anxiety disorder for a long time, but, knock on wood, I don't think I have it anymore. Or, at least, it's sub-clinical. I think my anxiety is incredibly well-ordered now. It shows up to meetings, it takes minutes, it behaves itself. It's a good dog.'

CHAPTER 14

A NEW PLAYER HAS ENTERED THE GAME

On May 12, 2008, Jim Brown, my uncle, killed himself. No matter how many times I write that sentence down it still shocks me. But there is another sentence, one which, no matter how many times I write it down, warms my heart and makes that first combination of words feel less all-consuming. On September 23, 2018, my daughter Lily May was born.

She's a wee cracker and, despite being a 'pleasant surprise', I now cannot imagine my life without her. Jenny and I had been together for ten years when Lily May was conceived but were living apart as a result of my work commitments. Writing full-time for *PC Gamer*, I was based at their headquarters in Bath, while Jenny remained in Glasgow. For the first six months of my time down south, I flew home most weekends. Talking on the phone and spending so little time together midweek admittedly put a strain on our relationship, which meant we spent a small but distinct portion of our Friday to Sunday reunions arguing, our situational frustrations bubbling over. Quite often, we allowed these petty squabbles to comandeer most of our first night together, which would make the three day stay feel even shorter than it already was.

Looking back, it was an unworkable situation – one which inevitably made even less sense when we found out Jenny was pregnant. I'd been home for the Christmas break of 2017 for a full two weeks when, on January 7, 2018, a few hours before I was due to fly back down to Bath, Jenny returned from the bathroom with a pregnancy test. It was positive. We tried another one. The same. And another. The same again. And then I had to leave. We'd hardly had time to process the news – is that *really* a blue line on the pee stick and are you *absolutely* sure? – far less absorb the magnitude of it.

Upon travelling back from Glasgow to Bath each week – via Bristol airport and a subsequent hour-long bus journey to Bath town centre – my dad often, very kindly, drove me from his house to Glasgow airport. On this occasion, I should have taken a taxi. My head was swimming, I needed space, and for whatever reason my mum joined us on this particular trip. I sat vacantly in the passenger seat of my dad's Chrysler Cruiser, shell-shocked, offering one word answers and politely nodding and shaking my head as each vacant gap in the conversation allowed. I played *Zelda: Breath of the Wild* on the plane and couldn't help but draw crude and pretentious comparisons between protagonist Link's journey into the game's vast new and unknown world, and the very real adventure I was set to embark on later that year. I've since finished *Breath of the Wild*, and for the avoidance of doubt I can confirm Link doesn't once change a shitey nappy at two in the morning, nor does he find himself fumbling around the kitchen in the dark making up bottles of water and powdered milk in the wee hours.

When I was back in Bath I attempted to get my head around what was great, if unexpected and life-changing news. In order to save money for our imminent arrival, Jenny and I agreed I'd return from England less regularly, after I'd informed my bosses of our situation and, hopefully, agreed that I could continue to work my job from Glasgow on a remote basis. They did, and I planned a move north during the first week in April. Jenny had it worse, for sure – her body was changing at a rate of knots, and I regret missing the first trimester of her pregnancy to this day – but I also learned living in a studio apartment in a different country from your loved ones, albeit England and a short flight away, can be really quite isolating. Nice as my colleagues were, I didn't spend any time with them outside of work, except the odd pizza night here and there, which meant I doubled-down on distractions. Occasionally, this meant going to the gym, but mostly it meant grabbing a pint at the Irish bar on the corner when the football was on and, of course, playing video games.

I threw myself into comfort games to combat the transient loneliness – games that I'd played years previously, that I understood and that didn't demand too much brain power after long days in the office. I played Rocksteady Studios' *Batman: Arkham City*, Kojima Productions' *Metal Gear Solid V: The Phantom Pain*, Square Enix's *Tomb Raider* reboot, and an old

'90s favourite, Revolution Software's *Broken Sword: Shadow of the Templars.* In *Arkham City*, one of Batman's favourite moves when neutralising baddies at the scene of any given crime is clambering up the insides of air conditioning vents before pouncing from the shadows. On my second visit to Arkham I became so engrossed that I found myself idly staring at the roof vents in the gym, sweat pissing off me as I propelled myself back and forth on the rowing machine, and thinking: *I wonder if I could fit in there. I bet Batman could.* When scoping out enemy bases in *Metal Gear Solid V*, players can assign glowing orange markers above individual baddies' heads to keep track of them when things get heavy behind enemy lines. I in turn imagined the same coloured flags floating above the heads of the shoppers ahead of me in the queue at Sainsbury's. I can't tell you why. But I can tell you I kept a close eye on that old woman buying bananas the entire time. I bet she's handy with that brolly. Can't be too safe.

Tour guides and travel books will tell you that Bath has some lovely Roman Empire-era architecture, but to be honest, the only thing that struck me about the buildings dotted around the town centre was how easy Lara Croft would find clambering around their rooftops and sandstone gable ends. Even now, reading all of this back, my inner monologue projects the calm and sarcastic lilt of *Broken Sword's* lead character George Stobbart as it often did during my time living in Somerset. Perhaps it was the solitude of living on my own that made my mind work in this way towards the end of my stay down south, but whatever the cause, these moments of art imitating life – or, more likely, me projecting video games onto the mundanities of reality – have stuck with me and still make me smile.

I smiled more when Lily May was born months later of course. I grinned from ear to ear when I balanced a PlayStation 4 controller on her lap two days after she'd returned from the hospital. I beamed when, at three months old, she watched me play Insomniac Games' *Spider-Man* from the comfort of her baby rocker, giggling as I made Peter Parker swing from ledge to lintel across the Manhattan skyline. I can't explain the joy I felt when, last month, she took a fair chunk of health from Dr Robotnik at the end of Act 1 in *Sonic Mania* as she fervently mashed X on the control pad without restrain. I consider DMA Design's *Lemmings* the first video game I ever fell I love with after my dad introduced me to the 2D puzzler via our family's first home computer, the Atari ST that he bought second-hand from the Barras Market in Glasgow. Some of my earliest and fondest fully-formed memories with my dad involve us hunched over the rear projection monitor together, trying to work out how to get the game's green haired, blue robed critters from A to B with minimal casualties. It felt serendipitous then when Jenny and Lily spent their first overnight together in hospital, I came home to grab clothes and get washed, and the *Lemmings* soundtrack played randomly on my Spotify shuffle while I was in the shower. Again, I smiled.

The birth of my daughter marks the most recent major milestone of my life, and through her I find myself looking to the future more than ever before. As a first time parent, I imagine that's natural. Jenny, Lily May and I now have our own house in Glasgow, and we are making our first memories as a family together. From here, I think about the things that will inevitably shape the course of Lily's life, and I think about how big a part video games played in mine over the years. As father and daughter, I wonder what our *Lemmings* moment will be, what game we'll sit in front of, making notes with pen and paper and helping each other through the toughest levels. Maybe I'll invite Granda Joe over to mark that occasion, three generations of Donnellys, each with a control pad in hand. I think I will.

I suspect Lily May will become a gamer of sorts through my influence but I wonder if she'll go as deep as me, if she'll live parts of her life through games or if she'll turn to them in times of crisis. I hope she doesn't experience the mental health issues I have but I hope that books like this one, and games like the ones written about within, can offer help and hope should she ever need them.

If ever there was a metaphor for my own mental health journey, it's *Checkpoint*. From Jim's suicide, to my deep depression and anxiety disorder that followed, suicidal thoughts, throwing myself into video games, seeking professional help, discovering the wave of independent adventures that examine and challenge mental illness, exploring the mental health communities in big-budget games such as *Grand Theft Auto V* and *EVE: Online,* and, ultimately, writing this book – I see my life, in terms of video games and mental health, as a series of milestones and checkpoints. In video games, checkpoints are landmarks which save your progress and mark your achievements and progression. I'm not a mental health professional but through the lens of mental health, checkpoints are a chance to pause and reflect on your emotional wellbeing. From *FIFA* to *Fortnite*, *Castlevania* to *Call of Duty*, *Mario Kart* to *Minecraft*, *Tetris* to *Tekken*; whether you play on PC, console, handheld, or your mobile phone; whether you consider yourself a casual or hardcore gamer, it doesn't matter how you play and enjoy video games. Video games are a brilliant learning tool, a means to bond with friends, family and strangers – either locally in person, or within sprawling, fantastical worlds online. They're a portal for escapism, or just a place to just chill out after a long week at school, at college, at work or in life in general. Video games can make us laugh and cry, they can make us feel love and anger, they can help us to grow and see the world from a different point of view. Video games can power up our minds, kick ass and save lives. They helped save mine, after all. And if you have related to anything contained within these pages, I firmly believe that they can help you too.

GLOSSARY

AAA or **"Triple A"** – a Triple A game is usually a game released by a major studio, with significant developmental and marketing budgets, expected to become one of the year's biggest and bestselling games

Avatar – an icon or figure that represents and identifies a player

CBT – cognitive behavioural therapy

Crunch – an often short-term, but sometimes long-term state of working where game developers at large companies are asked to work extended extra hours to meet deadlines, often without extra pay

DLC – Downloadable Content: additional new game content that becomes available usually months after a game's initial release that the player must download to access. Can be a new story mission, map, character features and more

DM – Direct message: a private message shared between two or more users which cannot be seen publicly by any other players

Esports – (also known as e-sports, eSports) a form of sport competition using video games. Esports often takes the form of organised, multiplayer video game competitions, particularly between professional players, individually or as teams.

Grind/Grinding – performing repetitive tasks, usually for a gameplay advantage or loot, but in some cases for purely aesthetic or cosmetic benefits in-game

Let's Play – the video documentation of a playthrough of a game, often from beginning to end, either recorded or live streamed by people on video platforms such as Twitch or YouTube, usually with commentary

Loot box/crate – a consumable virtual item which can be redeemed through specific gameplay to receive a randomised selection of further virtual items

MMORPG – massively multiplayer online role-playing game

Oculus Quest – brand name for an all-in-one gaming system for virtual reality, created by Facebook

Permadeath – a situation in which a character cannot reappear after having been killed and entire save files may be deleted

Platformer/Platform game – a type of video game featuring two-dimensional graphics where the player controls a character jumping or climbing between solid platforms at different positions on the screen

Sandbox – a game type in which there is no set objective or goals and players have freedom to create their own, at their own pace

Shooter – a genre of video game that is primarily focused on the mechanic of shooting other characters or players

ENDNOTES

FOREWORD

1. "Lockdown and loaded: coronavirus triggers video game boost." *BBC News*, 2020, www.bbc.co.uk/news/business-52555277.
2. @footballmanager. "Your free fornight – #FM20 data from the last two, free weeks. Thanks for your support, we hope you can continue to enjoy the journey you started" *Twitter*, 1 Apr. 2020, 7:01 p.m., twitter.com/footballmanager/status/12454108-51516903424.

INTRODUCTION: A PLAYER HAS LEFT THE GAME

1. Reshoeft, Christian. "How Our Flash Game Reached 18 Million Monthly Players In Two Years." *Miniclip*, 2013, blog.miniclip.com/2013/02/21/8-ball-pool-story/.
2. Reyes, Mariel Soto. "Esports Ecosystem Report 2020: The key industry players and trends growing the esports market which is on track to surpass $1.5B by 2023." *Business Insider*, 2019, www.businessinsider.com/esports-ecosystem-market-report.
3. Kelly, Andy. "Black Mirror creator Charlie Brooker on the reaction to its first interactive episode." *PC Gamer*, 2019, www.pcgamer.com/black-mirror-creator-charlie-brooker-on-the-reaction-to-its-first-interactive-episode/.
4. Judge, Alysia. "Video games and mental health: 'Nobody's properly talking'." *BBC News*, 2018, www.bbc.co.uk/news/newsbeat-44662669.

CHAPTER 1: A NEW JOURNEY

1. "Suicide: two lives lost in Scotland each day is a tragedy." *Mental Health Foundation*. www.mentalhealth.org.uk/campaigns/preventing-suicide-scotland.
2. "Suicide: Scottish trends." *ScotPHO Public Health Information for Scotland*, 2019, www.scotpho.org.uk/health-wellbeing-and-disease/suicide/data/scottish-trends/.
3. ibid
4. "Suicides in the UK: 2018 registrations." *Office for National Statistics*, 2019, www.ons.gov.uk/peoplepopulationandcommunity/birthsdeathsandmarriages/deaths/bulletins/suicidesin-the unitedkingdom/2018registrations.
5. "Suicide: Scottish trends." *ScotPHO Public Health Information for Scotland*, 2019, www.scotpho.org.uk/health-wellbeing-and-disease/suicide/data/scottish-trends/.
6. "Suicide facts and figures." *Samaritans*. www.samaritans.org/scotland/about-samaritans/research-policy/suicide-facts-and-figures/.
7. "2019 Essential facts about the computer and video game industry." *Entertainment Software Association*, 2019, https://www.theesa.com/esa-research/2019-essential-facts-about-the-computer-and-video-game-industry/.
8. "Scottish gamers spend over £400 on video games each year." *The Sunday Post*, 2018, www.sundaypost.com/fp/scottish-gamers-spend-over-400-on-video-games-each-year/.
9. "The games industry in numbers." *The Association for UK Interactive Entertainment*, 2018, https://ukie.org.uk/research.
10. Mahar, Ian. "Nobody Wins When Horror Games Stigmatize Mental Illness." *Kotaku*, 2013, kotaku.com/nobody-wins-when-horror-games-stigmatize-mental-illness-912462538.
11. "Crunch Hurts: How Unmitigated Overwork Harms Employee Health, Productivity, And Your Studio's Bottom Line." *Take This*, www.takethis.org/programs/industry-research/crunch-hurts/
12. "EA: The Human Story." *Live Journal*, 2004, ea-spouse.livejournal.com/274.html.

13. Surette, Tim. "EA settles OT dispute, disgruntled "spouse" outed." *Game Spot*, 2006, www.gamespot.com/articles/ea-settles-ot-dispute-disgruntled-spouse-outed/1100-6148369/.

14. "Wives of Rockstar San Diego employees have collected themselves." *Gamasutra*, 2010, www.gamasutra.com/blogs/RockstarSpouse/20100107/4032/Wives_of_Rockstar_San_Diego_employees_have_collected_themselves.php.

15. Campbell, Colin. "How Fortnite's success led to months of intense crunch at Epic Games." *Polygon*, 2019, www.polygon.com/2019/4/23/18507750/fortnite-work-crunch-epic-games.

16. Schreier, Jason. "Inside Rockstar Games' Culture Of Crunch." *Kotaku*, 2018, kotaku.com/inside-rockstar-games-culture-of-crunch-1829936466.

17. Schreier, Jason. "How BioWare's Anthem Went Wrong." *Kotaku*, 2019, kotaku.com/how-biowares-anthem-went-wrong-1833731964.

A NEW CHALLENGER APPEARS (JOHNNY CHIODINI)

1. "Mental health facts and statistics." *Mind*, www.mind.org.uk/information-support/types-of-mental-health-problems/statistics-and-facts-about-mental-health/how-common-are-mental-health-problems/

2. "Adult Psychiatric Morbidity in England – 2007, Results of a household survey." *National Centre for Social Research* and *the Department of Health Sciences, University of Leicester*, 2009, digital.nhs.uk/data-and-information/publications/statistical/adult-psychiatric-morbidity-survey/adult-psychiatric-morbidity-in-england-2007-results-of-a-household-survey.

CHAPTER 4: SOBERING EXPERIENCES

1. Thompson, Warren. "Alcoholism Clinical Presentation." *Medscape*, 2018,https://emedicine.medscape.com/article/285913-clinical#b1.
2. "Alcohol facts and figures". *Alcohol Focus Scotland*, www.alcohol-focus-scotland.org.uk/alcohol-information/alcohol-facts-and-figures/.

CHAPTER 5: A QUEST FOR HELP

1. Moss, Rachel. "41% Of Men Still Don't Seek Mental Health Support When They Need It." *Huffington Post*, 2019, www.huffingtonpost.co.uk/entry/41-of-men-still-dont-seek-mental-health-support-when-they-need-it_uk_5c8fb297e4b071a25a84f241?.&guccounter=1.
2. Bromley, Catherine; Dowling, Shanna; Gray, Linsay; Hughes, Tracey; Leyland, Alistair H; McNeill, Geraldine; Marcinkiewicz, Anna. "The Scottish Health Survey." *National Statistics*, 2014, www.gov.scot/Resource/0046/00464858.pdf.

CHAPTER 6: WHO AND YOU

1. "Share of leisure time spent playing video games in selected countries worldwide as of May 2016." *Statista Research Department*, 2016, www.statista.com/statistics/259306/distribution-of-time-playing-video-games-by-genre/.
2. Yin-Poole, Wesley. "It's time to stop running from gaming addiction." *Eurogamer*, 2019, www.eurogamer.net/articles/2018-06-27-gaming-addiction.
3. "Country's top mental health nurse warns video games pushing young people into 'under the radar' gambling." *NHS England*, 2020, www.england.nhs.uk/2020/01/countrys-top-mental-health-nurse-warns-video-games-pushing-young-people-into-under-the-radar-gambling/.
4. Zendle David, and Paul Cairns. "Video game loot boxes are linked to problem gambling: Results of a large-scale survey."

PLOS ONE, 13(11), e0206767. 21 Nov. 2018. Web.

5. Zendle, David, and Paul Cairns. "Loot Box Spending in Video Games Is Linked to Problem Gambling Severity." *PsyArXiv*, 14 Sept. 2018. Web.

6. "Loot boxes within video games." *Gambling Commission, 2017,* www.gamblingcommission.gov.uk/news-action-and-statistics/ News/loot-boxes-within-video-games.

7. *NHS England*, 8 October 2019, www.england.nhs.uk/2019/10/ children-treated-for-computer-gaming-addiction-under-nhs-long-term-plan/.

8. "UKIE LAUNCHES GET SMART ABOUT P.L.A.Y. – ESSENTIAL TOOLS FOR PARENTS." Safe in Our World, 2020, safeinourworld.org/news/ukie-launches-get-smart-about-p-l-a-y-essential-tools-for-parents/.

CHAPTER 8: A DEEP DIVE

1. "Understanding the facts of anxiety disorders and depression is the first step." Anxiety and Depression Association of America, adaa.org/understanding-anxiety.

2. Scott, Eric L and Leslie Hulvershorn. "Anxiety Disorders With Comorbid Substance Abuse." *Psychiatric Times*, 28(9), 7 Sept. 2011. Web.

3. "Mental health." *Director-General Health and Social Care/ Chief Executive of the NHS,* www.gov.scot/policies/mental-health/.

CHAPTER 9: 360 DEGREE THERAPY

1. "Mental health: facing the facts." *Poppy Scotland*, www.poppy-scotland.org.uk/unforgettable-stories/5245-2/.

2. Stallabrass, Julian. "Empowering Technology: The Exploration of Cyberspace." *New Left Review*, 211, May/June 1995. Web.

CHAPTER 13: FOR THE PLAYERS

1. "Esports Earnings: How Much Do Esports Players Make?" *JD Style*, blog.jdsports.co.uk/esports-earnings-how-much-do-players-really-make/.
2. "US teen wins $3 million at video game tournament Fortnite World Cup." *CNBC*, 2019, www.cnbc.com/2019/07/29/fortnite-world-cup-us-teen-wins-3-million-at-video-game-tournament.html.
3. Petrosyan, Albert. "Massive prize pool revealed for 2019 Call of Duty World Championship." *Dextero*, 2019, www.dexerto.com/call-of-duty/massive-prize-pool-revealed-for-2019-call-of-duty-world-championship-292774.
4. "Hearthstone announces $4 million prize pool in 2019." *ESPN*, 2018, www.espn.com/esports/story/_/id/2541-0787/hearthstone-announces-4-million-prize-pool-2019.
5. "The International 2019." *Liquipedia*, liquipedia.net/dota2/The_International/2019.
6. Iqbal, Mansoor. "Fortnite Usage and Revenue Statistics (2019)." *Business of Apps*, 2019, www.businessofapps.com/data/fortnite-statistics/.
7. Pearce, James. "BT Spot's HDR Champions League broadcast breaks record." *IBC*, 2019, www.ibc.org/tech-advances/bt-sports-hdr-champions-league-broadcast-breaks-record/3926.article.
8. Webb, Kevin. "Ninja, the world's most popular gamer, makes $500,000 every month playing Fortnite – here's how he does it." *Business Insider*, 2020, www.businessinsider.com/ninja-tyler-blevins-twitch-subscribers-fortnite-drake-youtube-20183?r=US&IR=T.
9. *Esports Earnings*, www.esportsearnings.com/players/female-players.
10. *Esports Earnings*, 2019, www.olbg.com/us/insights/esports-earnings
11. *ibid*.
12. Cooper, Edward and Annie Hayes. "Everything You Need to Know About Esports, Where Players Earn Up to £1,000,000 for Winning a Video Game." *Men's Health*, 2019, www.menshealth.com/uk/fitness/lifestyle/a28538491/esports/.

13. "How to Become a Pro Game in 10 Steps." *Intel*, www.intel.co.uk/content/www/uk/en/gaming/resources/want-pro-gamer.html.

14. Marelić, Marko and Dino Vukušić. "E-sports: Definition and social implications. Exercise and Quality of Life." 2019. 11. 47-54. 10.31382/eqol.191206. Web.

15. Arumuham, Atheeshaan. "8 ways esports players can improve their wellbeing and performance." *British Esports Association*, 2019, britishesports.org/advice/8-tips-esports-players-wellbeing-performance/.

LIST OF FEATURED GAMES

Here you will find all the games that were mentioned in case you fancy trying them out for yourself. They are listed in order of game, year of publication, genre and the following key will tell you what platforms they're available to play on. (Some platforms are not listed as they are obsolete or unavailable).

	PlayStation	Xbox	Nintendo Switch
	★	◻	⌘
	PC/Mac/Linux	Web Browser	Mobile (iOS/Android)
	◆	●	◼

8 Ball Pool	2010	pool simulation	●◼
Actual Sunlight	2014	interactive story	◆
Adventures with Anxiety	2019	interactive story	●
Alan Wake	2010	action adventure, survival	◻◆
Amnesia: The Dark Descent	2010	horror adventure, survival	◆
Among The Sleep	2015	horror adventure, survival	◻◆
Angry Birds	2009	casual puzzle game	◆◼

Animal Crossing: Pocket Camp	2017	social simulation ■	
Animal Crossing: New Horizons	2020	social simulation ⌘	
Anthem	2019	multiplayer action RPG ◆★□	
Assassin's Creed	2016	action adventure ★□◆	
Astroneer	2016	sandbox adventure ★□◆	
Batman: Arkham City	2011	action adventure ★□◆	
BioShock	2007	first-person shooter ★□⌘◆■	
Bloodborne	2015	action RPG ★	
Braid	2008	puzzle platformer ★□◆■	
Broken Sword: Shadow of the Templars	1996	point & click adventure ★◆■	
Call of Duty	2003	first-person shooter ★□◆■	
Candy Crush	2012	puzzle ●■	
Castlevania	1986 – present	action adventure ★□◆	
Celeste	2018	platformer ★□⌘◆	
Coin Master	2018	casual adventure ■	
Coming Out Sim	2014	interactive story ●	
Countdown	1990	adventure ◆	
Counter-Strike: Global Offensive	2012	multiplayer first-person shooter ★□◆	
Crash Bandicoot	1996 – present	platformer ★	
Dark Souls	2012	action RPG ★□⌘◆	
Darkest Dungeon	2016	action RPG ★□⌘◆	
Dead Cells	2017	action platformer ★□⌘◆	
Deep	TBC	VR therapy	

Depression Quest	2013	interactive story ♦
Don't Starve	2013	survival ⋆□⌘♦■
Dota 2	2013	multiplayer online battle ♦
Elder Sign	2011	board game ♦■
EVE Online	2003	MMORPG space sim ♦
Farmville	2009	casual simulation ●■
Fatal Frame 4	2008	horror survival (Wii)
FIFA	1993 – present	sport simulation ⋆□⌘♦■
Fixation	2012	puzzle platformer ●
Football Manager	2019	sport simulation ⋆□⌘♦■
Forget Me Not:		
My Organic Garden	2015	point & click story ♦■
Fortnite	2017	battle royale ⋆□⌘♦■
Faster Than Light	2012	strategy ♦■
Gone Home	2013	adventure mystery ⋆□⌘♦
Grand Theft Auto V	2013	open world action ⋆□♦
Guitar Hero	2005	music rhythm ⋆□♦■
Hearthstone	2014	card game ♦■
Hitman: Codename 47	2000	stealth action ♦
Hollow Knight	2017	action adventure ⋆□⌘♦
Journey	2012	adventure ⋆♦
Layers of Fear	2016	psychological horror ⋆□⌘♦
League of Legends	2009	multiplayer battle arena ♦
Lemmings	1991	puzzle platformer ♦
Life Is Strange	2015	adventure ⋆□♦
Limbo	2010	puzzle platformer ⋆□⌘♦■
Little Red Lie	2017	adventure ⋆♦■

Mass Effect:

Andromeda	2017	action RPG ★□◆
Max Payne 3	2012	first person shooter ★□◆
Metal Gear Solid	1987 – present	action stealth ★□◆
Minecraft	2009	sandbox survival ◆
Missile Command	1980	arcade shoot 'em up
Mount & Blade	2010	action strategy RPG ◆
NBA 2K20	2019	sport simulation ★□⌘◆
Need for Speed	1994 – present	racing ★□◆
Neverending		
Nightmares	2013	survival horror ◆■
Outlast	2013	survival horror ★□⌘◆
Overcooked	2016	cooking simulation ★□⌘◆
Overwatch	2015	multiplaer shooter ★□⌘◆
Papers, Please	2013	puzzle simulation ★◆
Papo & Yo	2012	puzzle adventure ★◆
Parables of the		
Polygons	2014	interactive story ●
Pong	1972	arcade sport simulation
Pro Evolution Soccer	1995 – present	sport simulation ★□◆
Red Dead		
Redemption	2010	action adventure ★□
Red Dead		
Redemption 2	2018	action adventure ★□◆
Resident Evil 2	1998/2019	survival horror ★□◆
Retro/Grade	2012	rhythm shoot 'em up ★◆
Ring Fit Adventure	2019	exercise action RPG ⌘
Rocket League	2015	sport simulation ★□⌘◆

Sanitarium	1998	adventure ◆■
Sea of Thieves	2016	action adventure □◆
Sekiro	2019	action adventure ★□◆
Silent Hill	1999 – present	survival horror ★□◆
SimCity	1989 – 2014	city-building simulator ★□◆
Slime Rancher	2016	open world adventure ★□◆
Sonic Mania	2017	platformer ★□⌘◆
Sonic the Hedgehog	1991	platformer ⌘◆■
Space Harrier	1985	rail shooter
Spelunky	2013	platformer ★□◆
Spider-Man	2018	action adventure ★
Spyro The Dragon	1998	platformer ★
Street Fighter 2	1993	arcade fight sim
Star Wars Battlefront II	2017	first person shooter ★□◆
Subnautica	2014	open world survival ★□◆
Suikoden	1995	RPG ★
Super Mario Bros	1985	platformer (Nintendo system)
Super Mario Odyssey	2017	action adventure platformer ⌘
Super Meat Boy	2010	platformer ★□⌘◆
Teamfight Tactics	2019	auto battler ◆■
Team Fortress 2	2007	first person shooter ★□◆
Tekken	1994 – 2017 (latest)	arcade action ★□◆
Tetris	1984	puzzle
Texas HoldeEm Poker	2009	poker simulation ●■
The Company of Myself	2009	puzzle platformer ●
The Elder Scrolls IV: Oblivion	2006	open world action RPG ★□◆

The Elder Scrolls		
V: Skyrim	2011	open world action RPG ★□⌘♦
The Evil Within	2014	horror survival ★□♦
The Institute	1983	adventure
The Legend of Zelda:		
Breath of the Wild	2017	action adventure ⌘
The Long Dark	2017	survival ★□♦
The Shattering	2019	first person shooter ★♦
The Sims	2000 – present	life simulation ★□♦
The Stanley Parable	2013	interactive story ♦
The Town of Light	2016	adventure ★□⌘♦
The Walking Dead	2012	interactive story ★□⌘♦
The Witcher 3	2015	action RPG ★□⌘♦
Theme Park	1994	construction sim ★♦
Tomb Raider	1996	action adventure ★♦
Toy Story 2	1999	platformer ★♦
Uncharted 2	2009	action adventure ★
World of Warcraft	2004	action MMORPG ♦
Wreck-It Ralf	2012	platformer ■
XCOM 2	2016	turn-based strategy ★□⌘♦
XCOM: Enemy		
Unknown	1994	turn-based strategy ★♦

ACKNOWLEDGEMENTS

I couldn't have written this book without the help, support, inspiration and encouragement of the following people. I earnestly thank:

The multi-talented Laura Jones and Heather McDaid from publisher 404 Ink for your vision, enthusiasm and commitment to *Checkpoint* – from start to finish, pitch to manuscript, you've both been great. Thanks to Laura for your editorial wisdom, direction, fine eye for detail, and for bringing clarity to my ramblings and believing wholeheartedly in the book's message.

Leah McDowell of ELEMdesign for her stunning cover artwork, which I fell in love with at first sight.

All the video game developers, video game players, and mental health professionals who contributed to and informed this book. One of the most inspiring things about writing is speaking to people who love what they do, and I hope I captured your enthusiasm within these pages. Keep doing what you're doing, keep changing the world, and keep underscoring the value of video games.

My daughter Lily May for inspiring me every single day. I've never known love like the love I have for you, and I can't wait to watch you grow up and, hopefully, play video games with yer auld da. At this point, you're already better than me at *Sonic Mania*. And I suspect you're just getting started.

My uncle Jim. Without you this book wouldn't exist. I wish it didn't, of course, but I think you'd be proud of me if only you could see me now. I can't tell you to your face how much you were and are loved, but I sincerely hope you've found peace wherever you are. I'll pop up to St Conval's and read it to you and my granny at some point – the eternal opportunist in me is determined to take advantage of a captive audience.

My mum and dad, Jackie and Joe, for pretty much everything. For raising me, loving me, believing in me, encouraging me, supporting me, being my best friends and for buying the Atari ST computer that set me on this long and winding, weird and wonderful path. Thank you for humouring my incessant video game chatter from a young age, and for pretending to understand why *Final Fantasy 8* is better than *Final Fantasy 7*, but not as good as *Suikoden 2*.

My in-laws – Phil and Michael senior, for making me feel like part of your family from day one; Michael junior, Lisa, Anne and Gareth, for showing me love, giving me friendship and treating me like your brother; and to wee Ellie for being the best wee niece and pal to Lily May.

My best mates Grant and Richie, with whom I've shared the shite patter and stories reflected in this book with for 30 (!) years.

And most of all, my fiancé, Jenny. Thank you for putting up with me, for inspiring me, for loving me, for encouraging me, for believing in me, and for picking me up off the ground and telling it like it is when I needed to hear it. Thanks for being a fantastic mother to our wonderful daughter, a brilliant partner and for the furious determination with which you play *Sonic the Hedgehog*, all the while assuring me that, yes, you *do* need to collect *every single* ring in Greenhill Zone, actually.

ABOUT JOE DONNELLY

Joe Donnelly is a Glaswegian journalist, writer, video games enthusiast and mental health advocate. He has written about both subjects' complex intersections for the *Guardian*, *New Statesman*, *VICE*, *PC Gamer* and many more, and believes the interactive nature of video games makes them uniquely placed to educate and inform.

You can follow him on Twitter at @deaco2000.

If you need someone to talk to Samaritans are a mental health charity and service
for crisis and support.

Whatever you're going through,
you can contact Samaritans in any way below:

Phone: call from any phone on 116 123.
It's free, one-to-one and open 24 hours a day.

Email: jo@samaritans.org
and they will respond to you as soon as they can.

Write:
Chris,
Freepost RSRB-KKBY-CYJK,
PO Box 9090,
Stirling,
FK8 2SA.

They aim to reply within 7 days.

More information: samaritans.org